D0986833

HEIST!

John F. Blair, Publisher   Winston-Salem, North Carolina

HEIST!

The $17 Million Loomis Fargo Theft

Jeff Diamant

Published by John F. Blair, Publisher

The paper in this book meets the guidelines
for permanence and durability of the
Committee on Production Guidelines for
Book Longevity of the Council on Library Resources

Library of Congress Cataloging-in-Publication Data
Diamant, Jeff, 1972–
Heist! : The $17 million Loomis Fargo theft / by Jeff Diamant.
p. cm.
Includes index.
ISBN 0-89587-252-8
1. Larceny—North Carolina—Charlotte. 2. Loomis, Fargo & Co.
3. Criminal investigation—North Carolina—Charlotte. I. Title.
HV6661.N82 1997 .D5 2002
364.16'2'0975676—dc21
2002010016

Book design by Debra Long Hampton

CONTENTS

HEIST!

Author's Note

This book combines information from interviews, trial testimony, field trips, FBI documents, and court papers concerning the $17 million theft from Loomis, Fargo & Co. I interviewed almost every major person involved in the heist and its investigation, the notable exception being Steve Chambers, many of whose relevant views and actions were publicly known or were available through court documents and his trial testimony.

Most of the important information gleaned from individual interviews was corroborated through interviews with other people. On the infrequent occasions when accounts differed, I resolved matters through available court documents and further interviews.

Teamwork

"DON'T DOUBLE-CROSS US," the woman on the phone told David Ghantt. "Don't back out on us. Steve's a serious guy."

Her tone pissed him off. Who was she to be pushing David around? *Steve* was a serious guy? It was David who was hours away from committing the most daring act of his life, and she was going off about *Steve* being a serious guy?

"I don't give a fuck," David told her. And with that, he hung up the phone at Loomis, Fargo & Co., his soon-to-be ex-employer in Charlotte, North Carolina. It was two o'clock in the afternoon on October 4, 1997, and there was tension between two planners of what would be the second-largest cash heist in United States history.

The woman on the phone was Kelly Jane Campbell, and David had a mad crush on her. She had attitude. Spunk. A parrot tattoo on her right ankle. She was five-foot-seven and had dirty-blond hair. They had worked together about a year at Loomis Fargo, until Kelly left for

Kelly Campbell knew David Ghantt from their time working together at Loomis, Fargo & Co.
John D. Simmons / CHARLOTTE OBSERVER

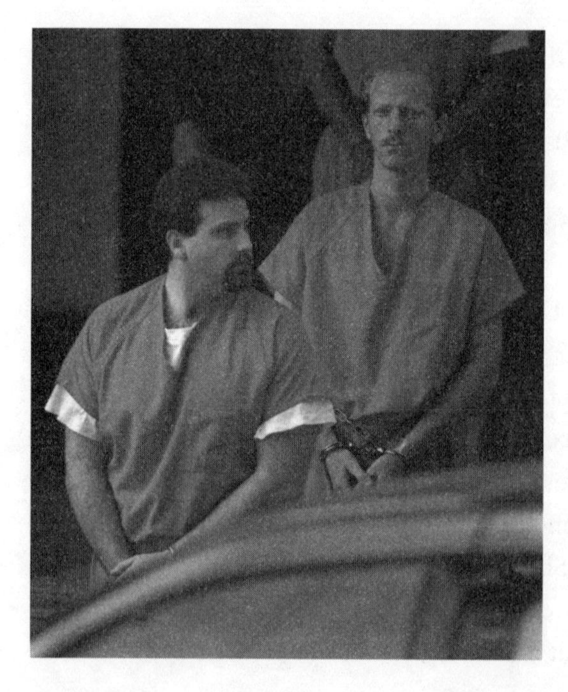

Steve Chambers (left) and David Ghantt never laid eyes on each other until after David had stolen $17 million from Loomis, Fargo & Co. and passed it to a group led by Steve.
CHARLOTTE OBSERVER

another job in 1996, but they stayed in touch. Now, they were poised to attempt a crime like almost no other.

Kelly had approached David with the idea in the summer, winning him over with the promise that a friend of hers with a shady background, including Mafia ties, would help them. The friend's name was Steve, and Kelly said he knew his way around the crime world. David and Steve had not met, but Steve already had secured him somebody else's birth certificate and social security card, which Kelly passed to him. David and Kelly had driven to Rock Hill, South Carolina, and used the documents—which belonged to a man named Mike McKinney—to obtain a fake ID that David planned to live on later.

David did not know Steve's last name. That was planned. If the shit came down, the planners would not be able to identify each other to the police. It echoed the movie *Reservoir Dogs*, in which the pawns in the robbery knew each other only by names like Mr. Blue and Mr. Pink.

Agitated, David returned to work after hanging up on Kelly. The only employee with him on this day was a Loomis Fargo trainee. David was supposed to be showing him the ropes of a job that included cash pickups and deliveries. Loomis Fargo, the nation's largest privately held armored-car company, used vans to transport hundreds of millions of dollars a day belonging to banks and other businesses, stocking automated teller machines and keeping money in the Loomis vault until it was time to move it.

The trainee did not yet know how the place worked. David planned to use this to his advantage.

The phone rang at about 2:20. It was Kelly again. "Everything's gonna be all right," she told him.

The plan was still on, but David remained steamed. "Just remind Steve," he said, "that I might be trouble my *own* self."

There was harmony between them now. David, calm, said he

needed her to drive to Loomis before the theft that night to take a duffel bag out of his parked pickup truck. It had his cell phone and handgun. It was unlocked for her. He told her he thought he would be able to send the trainee home at about six o'clock and would need about an hour to load the money—which was on the floor and on carts and on shelves—into a company van.

"Do you know how much there's gonna be?" she asked.

"About $14 million or $15 million," he said. He would be ready about seven o'clock.

When they hung up, she called his pager, leaving the code 143, which David knew to mean "I love you," because *I* has one letter, *love* has four, and *you* has three.

David would empty the vault and deliver the money to the others. The loot would later be divided among David, Kelly, and Steve. David's share would be sent to Mexico, where he planned to hide and where he expected Kelly to join him.

David was an avid reader. As a child, he had preferred reading nonfiction books to playing sports. He would say that although he couldn't tell you who was on first, he knew who the Egyptian god of the dead was. As an adult, he liked reading Shakespeare, Tom Clancy, and anything about the Federal Bureau of Investigation.

He had just finished reading a book about the FBI and felt it gave him insight into how agents investigated, insight he thought could help his little gang get away with a grand heist. For example, knowing that the FBI could electronically trace a suspect's recent spending activity through bank papers, credit card records, and land transactions, he told Kelly they would have to control themselves and spend the money discretely.

"For the first year after a crime," he told her, "they're all over you, with six to ten agents. But after a year, they cut it down to two agents. And after two years, the case is just a file. If we can sit on the money for a year, maybe two, it could work."

Of course, they would need help before that in moving the stolen money to safety the night of the crime. David followed the news. He had heard about the man who recently committed the biggest armored-car-company heist in United States history. This guy was from Florida, a loner named Philip Noel Johnson, and he also had worked for Loomis. He stole $18.8 million in March 1997, only to be caught seven months later while crossing into Texas from Mexico to retrieve some of the money, which he had hidden in a shed in mountainous western North Carolina. A female customs inspector, asking routine questions of bus passengers, focused on him when he answered her in a tone reminiscent of Jon Lovitz's pathological-liar character from *Saturday Night Live.* Asked the purpose of his visit, Johnson replied, "To visit friends." The guard asked, "To visit friends?" Johnson said, "Yeah, that's it. To visit friends." Philip Noel Johnson was arrested.

"His problem," David told Kelly, "is that he did it alone."

David planned to leave the stolen money behind with his co-conspirators while he fled to Mexico. He would have the bulk of his share sent to him south of the border. If that did not work out, he could return to the United States at an appropriate time, under an assumed name.

But he hoped that Kelly would come live with him in Mexico, and that they would be lovers. She wanted the same thing, she said. They had not slept together, or even fooled around, but he was ready to live with her. Their only intimate physical contact had been kissing on a mid-September night, when they had driven her pickup truck to a field behind a shooting range in Gaston County to talk about their plans and the theft's chance of success. David thought they had an 85 percent chance of getting away with it.

It may seem strange that David was willing to pass off millions of stolen dollars to people he didn't know extremely well—or even at all—but he placed a great deal of trust in the notion of teamwork. It was drilled into him in the army, when David repaired helicopters during the Persian Gulf War. "Gimme a team of five guys and I can do anything," he would say. David knew he would be the main suspect immediately because of his work schedule, but he believed that if he succeeded, his share of the loot would keep him comfortable the rest of his life. Yes, teamwork was the only way to go. He thought of Philip Noel Johnson's mistake in Florida. Teamwork was the answer.

Kelly and David had known each other for two years. In December 1995, on one of her first days at Loomis, goofy David walked up to her inside the chain-link fence that surrounded the building. "If you give me a cigarette, I'll be your friend," David said with a flirty smile.

"I don't need any more friends," she shot back. "But you can still have a cigarette."

David got a kick out of the blunt woman. He could talk to her about anything, about things he couldn't discuss with his wife. NASCAR. Four-wheeling. How he felt shorted by life. How he and his wife had trouble communicating. Kelly thought he was funny and laughed at things he said.

David wanted to be more than friends with Kelly, who also was married, but she wanted to keep things platonic.

She left Loomis in November 1996, taking a new post as a security guard. Afterwards, Kelly and David would talk only occasionally, over the phone. Their most important conversation occurred one afternoon in August 1997, after Kelly paged David at work. He called her back. They talked about his job, his life, his wife. They joked about Loomis and about how easy it would be to steal from the place.

Among Loomis employees, conversations about stealing from the company were not rare. For people earning $8.15 an hour—David's salary—the jokes came naturally.

But this time, on the phone, Kelly wasn't joking. "Just think about it," she said. "What would it take to make you do it?"

Over the next two weeks, David thought about it. Living with his wife, Tammy, in a mobile home, he longed for the relatively luxurious middle-class lifestyle of his childhood, which included Disney World vacations, a religious-school education, and nicer shopping trips than he could afford as a self-supporting adult. When he was growing up, his mother took him shopping at the mall, to Sears, to J. C. Penney. As a man, he shopped at Wal-Mart. He knew there was nothing wrong with shopping at Wal-Mart, but he wished he could afford other options.

He even had to watch what he bought at the grocery store. They could have one or two meals each week that he really liked, but the rest were hot dogs or Hamburger Helper. He was on a budget for clothes. Even for work boots. Only recently, he had checked seven stores before finding work boots in his price range. The prosperity of Charlotte's booming metropolitan area was all around him, and he felt left out.

He thought it was unfair. He was a hard worker. He was smart enough. He had graduated from high school and joined the army. He earned an honorable discharge, but because of defense-industry cutbacks across the country, he could not find a good job. He lacked a college degree, and his army skills seemed meaningless in the job market of the 1990s.

He married Tammy in 1992 and earned low wages fueling airplanes at the airport in Hilton Head, South Carolina. In 1994, they moved to Gastonia, where they had grown up, and David took a job driving a forklift. Later that year, he saw a newspaper ad for a job at Loomis Fargo. He put on his best pair of jeans, a button-down shirt, and his nicest cowboy boots. The supervisor liked him. He got the job.

In Gastonia, he would run into people from his high school, people who had never struck him as especially smart. Their lives seemed far easier, far better than his. He could not understand why he wasn't more successful, why he couldn't at least match the success of his father, who earned a comfortable salary driving a truck.

It wasn't fair, he thought over and over again. He deserved more. Stealing from Loomis Fargo could make him rich, if he got away with it. He could be famous.

But thoughts of his wife and parents would give him pause. He would have to leave Tammy. And his mother would be traumatized.

Growing up, David was a decent student who was at worst a minor troublemaker and prankster. One night as a teenager, he and a friend stole a construction company's Porta-Jon, tied it to the back of a pickup truck, and drove around for about fifteen minutes. Then they put the Porta-Jon back. Another time, the day after a Christmas in the late 1980s, David and some friends planted all of the discarded Christmas trees in the area in one neighbor's front yard. When a prank seemed dangerous, David backed out. One time, some friends stole a stop sign from a busy intersection. David made them put it back.

But with Kelly's new idea on the table, he realized several things: he hated his job; he hated his bosses; he wasn't going to advance at Loomis; he'd lost hope in his marriage; he couldn't afford to quit work to get a college degree; he wasn't going to advance in life without doing something drastic.

He flip-flopped on the heist idea three or four times from late August to mid-September. Then, one day, David was reviewing his and Tammy's credit card bill. He did some quick math and realized that even if they met the minimum monthly payments, the bill would take thirty years to pay. And they could barely afford the minimum payments, given the power bills, phone bills, car insurance bills, and home payments they had to meet. David decided that if Kelly called again, he would go for it.

Sure enough, she called a few days later, around September 16. "What would it take to convince you to do it?" she asked.

"I'll need help moving the money, getting a new ID, and leaving the country," he told her.

"Are you serious?" Kelly asked.

He said he was.

Kelly didn't know if David meant it, but she blurted out, "I've got a friend who can hook you up with a new ID."

And just like that, David became a thief in the making.

The October 4 shift was lasting longer than expected, due to delays involving pickups and deliveries. As it neared its end, David stealthily left the vault door ajar. The trainee did not know to check it.

David and the trainee left the warehouse. In the parking lot, David sat in his pickup truck smoking a cigarette. When the trainee drove home, David waved. At about 6:40, he went back inside.

The walk-in vault was a fortified gray room, more wide than long, with shelves, cabinets, desks, and multiple pushcarts stocked with shrink-wrapped cash. Vans could pull up inside the building and next to the vault, so outsiders couldn't see money being loaded. In preparation for his plan, David had backed an unmarked company Ford Econoline van near the vault entrance and opened its back door.

His task was not easy. Though much of the money in the vault was already stacked on pushcarts when David began, other stacks were on shelves or the floor, and they were heavy. David was thin—six-foot-one, 165 pounds—and heaving the stacks onto the cart, pushing the cart toward the vault door, and emptying its contents into the van was exhausting. Beads of sweat formed under his red hair.

He didn't stop with one cart. He went back inside the vault, loaded up another cart, and repeated the process. Sweat began to darken his gray Loomis uniform. Seven o'clock came and went. Seven-twenty did, too. Kelly called, using David's own cell phone, to ask where the hell he was already, because she and the others were waiting outside for him.

"I'm busy," he said. "I don't have time to mess with you. I gotta go." He hung up on her.

He knew they were nervous waiting for him. He also knew he would not stop stealing until he had taken everything. Stealing even a

It took David Ghantt about an hour to remove all the money from the Loomis Fargo vault. He didn't realize the company would later have this view of him.
CHARLOTTE OBSERVER

small amount, he reasoned, broke the bond of trust between him and his company as surely as stealing millions. And in the grand scheme of things, if he got caught, the prison sentence for stealing $20 million wouldn't be much worse than for stealing just $500,000—maybe a few extra years behind bars.

Each cart, holding about $2 million, was taking seven or eight minutes to stack, push, and empty into the van, and there were about eight cartloads' worth in the vault. David did not rest until the vault was empty, at about seven forty-five.

When all the money was in the van, relief dulled the tension pulsing through his veins. The most daring task was done. But he was not finished. He closed the vault and set the security timer so the vault could not be opened for two or three days. He knew that would hinder the company's response, as would his possession of both existing sets of vault keys. Then he hurried into the manager's office, where three TV security screens and two VCRs were visible. David's bosses would know he had worked that day, and that he was missing, but without a video, maybe they would think he had been held up at gunpoint and taken hostage, or even better, killed. He ejected the two VCR tapes, which he knew had recorded images of him during the last hour. He took the tapes with him and prepared to leave.

He called Kelly to say he was coming. He hopped into the driver's seat of the loaded Loomis van. His plan was to drive out the building's electronic back gate, which consisted of horizontal metal plates that opened at the touch of a button. He would never be in the Loomis Fargo warehouse again, he realized.

The gate would not open.

His eyes widened with fear. His heart rate quickened. He could not believe it. Would he fail because of something as simple as this? Even if he didn't get away, he had done enough already that he would have to explain himself to his bosses, who would fire him and have him arrested. He tried again to make the back gate rise, but it wouldn't.

He called Kelly on the cell phone and relayed his predicament. What should he do? An idea came to them—David could exit through the building's front gate. Under this Plan B, once he was outside, he would also have to exit a chain-link fence surrounding that part of the building. And another factor would cause extra minutes of delay. If David was going to exit the front gate, he would have to move two other Loomis vans that were parked inside the building, blocking that gate. He got into each one, turned the ignition, and drove a few feet so his exit was unobstructed.

David sighed when the front gate rose. He drove the van outside and hopped out to open the chain-link fence. Free at last?

Nothing was coming easy. David couldn't open the chain-link fence. He pushed. He tugged. He pulled. Kelly and the others, in two waiting vehicles, watched and shook their heads in worry. The people in the vehicles began talking to each other via cell phone.

Help came from an unknown source. A black-haired man popped out of a Mazda 626 and approached the gate, twisting so David couldn't see his face. David wondered if the man was Steve.

There was no time for introductions. The man helped David swing open the gate. David drove the Loomis van out, and the man hustled back to the Mazda, where another, larger man waited. The three-vehicle caravan was ready. Kelly would lead in her pickup truck, David would follow in the Loomis van, and the Mazda would take the rear.

They drove down Suttle Avenue, passing grassy Bryant Park. To the right, between the park's trees, the thieves could have caught a glimpse of Charlotte's skyline of bank buildings in the twilight, about two miles away. It included the sixty-story NationsBank building and the slightly smaller First Union Bank building, headquarters for the two banks that rightfully owned most of the money David was driving into the night.

But the Charlotte skyline did not catch their attention. They headed down Morehead Street to Freedom Drive, a main road that passed industrial buildings, gas stations, and fast-food restaurants toward Interstate 85.

David pulled out a cigarette, put it in his mouth, and maneuvered his nondriving hand to light it.

He saw a Charlotte-Mecklenburg Police car in front of him.

He shuddered. He spit the unlit cigarette on to the floor and kept driving. If the cop stopped him, that would be it. Would the cop pull them over? What were the odds?

The unsuspecting police officer turned his car on to another road, leaving the caravan free to continue.

After two miles on Freedom Drive and then five more on I-85 South, the vehicles pulled off the interstate at the Sam Wilson Road exit and on to the two-lane Performance Road, a service road for industrial buildings. Those buildings included a printing business called

Reynolds & Reynolds, their next destination.

The gate of Reynolds & Reynolds opened for them. On a Saturday night, its parking lot was as good as a private warehouse. No one else was around.

Once inside the printing company's gate, the two men hopped out of the Mazda. David got out of the Loomis van, leaving his company handgun and the two security videotapes but taking with him a massive key ring that held about 125 keys. He gave the key ring to the man who had helped him open the chain-link fence. He placed the correct key for the Loomis van in the man's hand. Then David opened the passenger door of Kelly's pickup truck and hopped inside.

"Let's get out of here," he said.

Kelly drove back to I-85, and David's escape was under way. Kelly would drop him off at Columbia Metropolitan Airport in South Carolina. That was a ninety-minute drive. The group had assumed that security guards at the nearby Charlotte airport—ten minutes away—already would be looking for David, and that even if he were able to leave from there, the FBI would track down people using the airport that night, show them his picture, and find out what plane he took.

On the way to Columbia, the immensity of his actions began to hit him. He held out wads of the stolen cash, gripping green stacks that totaled a year's salary for him. "I'm richer with what's in my hand right now," he said, "than I've ever been." He changed out of his uniform.

They laughed together when Kelly said, "I'm a *rich* bitch now!"

David had taken about $50,000 as a first installment of his share, but he was not sure how he would sneak it into Mexico. He decided he couldn't get it all past airport security. Kelly had an idea. She suggested they stop at a convenience store and buy pantyhose. A snip here, a snip there, and David had a money belt. Twenty grand went into the belt. He stuffed $5,000 into his cowboy boots. Kelly took the rest. He threw away his credit cards and identification.

Back on the road, they soon approached the Columbia airport. It was about nine-thirty. While still in the truck, Kelly gave David the number for a pay telephone located outside the Country Lane Market, a convenience store in Mount Holly, a small North Carolina town just west of Charlotte. Kelly would wait there for his calls at one o'clock in the afternoon on Tuesdays and Thursdays.

David noticed that the airport seemed quiet. Kelly parked, and the two of them walked toward the terminal. David had not asked about his plane ticket during the drive, assuming that Kelly would just pull one out at the appropriate time, or at least that there would be a reservation for him. After all, if he was sticking his neck out stealing a zillion dollars, the very least his cohorts could do was complete the simple tasks of getting him a ticket and making sure he was driven to an airport that was open! But from the minute they parked, he feared the airport was closed. And it was. David did not yell. He didn't want to make a scene. Besides, he was stunned silent. How could his gang have screwed this part up for him? It placed their whole plan in serious jeopardy.

Kelly Campbell hoped to use money from the heist to move from this mobile home in Mount Holly, North Carolina, to a house with a pool. *John D. Simmons* / CHARLOTTE OBSERVER

Kelly called Steve from an airport pay phone. They decided David's fastest route to Mexico would be through Hartsfield International Airport in Atlanta.

Kelly didn't want to drive him there, and she didn't know how to find a bus station, so, from a Waffle House pay phone, she called a cab to take David to a bus. A quick kiss, a quick good-bye, and he was gone.

As he stared out the window on the bus to Atlanta, David reflected on what he had just done. It would change his life forever. He felt exhilarated. He would overcome the error with the airport, he thought.

Once in Atlanta, David sought a connection to Mexico. He found a flight to New Orleans, where he would be able to get an AeroMexico flight to Cancun.

His plane landed in Louisiana before dawn on October 5. He was disheveled and sweaty from the stress of the theft and the escape. He checked into a downtown hotel, turned the air conditioner on high, and clicked on the television news, expecting to see his face or hear his name. There was nothing about him or the theft, probably because it was too early in the morning, he figured. He was probably safe for the time being. He decided to catch a few hours of sleep before his flight to Cancun.

Rested, he took a cab back to the New Orleans airport, where his next moment of panic awaited. After checking in for his flight, he ordered a slice of pizza at a food court and sat down to eat. An elderly woman stared at him. He didn't stare back, but her look made him nervous. What was she staring at? He pretended not to notice her and started eating.

She approached him. "Hey, I think I know you!"

He stopped chewing. "Ma'am?"

"Yeah, I know who you are!"

"I don't think so, ma'am."

"You're, you're . . . Wait a minute."

David couldn't believe it. How could an old woman in Louisiana be foiling his escape so quickly?

"You're that tennis player! The German! Boris Becker!"

Relieved, David exhaled and recited from his fake ID. "I'm Mike," he said. "I'm in computer sales."

The old woman left. David's heartbeat returned to normal. He finished his food and boarded the plane, passing unsuspecting police officers with more than $25,000 around his waist and in his cowboy boots.

The plane took off. The plane landed. At the customs gate, the officer asked how long David would be in Mexico.

"Two weeks," he answered.

It was hot, and David was dressed for the North Carolina autumn. He found a cab outside the airport and hopped in. David's Spanish consisted mainly of "*por favor*" and "*cerveza*," the words for *please* and *beer*. He asked the cabdriver, in English, to take him to a hotel.

"Cheap or 'spensive?" the driver asked.

" 'Spensive is okay," David said.

He was on his way. The first part of the heist was a success. All he needed was for his co-conspirators in North Carolina to follow the plan.

How to Launder $150,000

IN HIS THIRTY YEARS OF LIFE, Steven Eugene Chambers had been a bookie, a tax cheat, and a loan shark, but he had never been into this kind of cash. Few criminals ever had.

For several hours after the theft on October 4, 1997, Steve's well-furnished mobile home near Lincolnton, North Carolina, about forty-five miles from Loomis Fargo, was Heist Central. It was where most of David Ghantt's accomplices counted the money while David fled the country, and it was Kelly's immediate destination after saying good-bye to him in Columbia.

Steve assumed control of the money about fifteen minutes after David stole it. He waited in his Mazda outside the Loomis Fargo building while David was inside stealing the money. His cousin Scott, one of two last-minute recruits Steve brought into the plan, was with him. Kelly waited nearby, alone in her pickup.

Steve stayed cool during most of the night's excitement and chaos.

When David was late coming out of the Loomis building, Scott asked nervously, "What's gonna happen if he don't come?"

Steve calmly answered, "He's coming, he's coming."

Twenty minutes later, when David couldn't open the front gate, Steve, after fielding a cell-phone call from Kelly, directed his cousin to help. When Scott protested, Steve said, "You have to. He can't do it alone." So Scott left the car and hustled to the gate, twisting his body so David Ghantt, if ever arrested, would not know what he looked like.

Steve's Mazda took up the rear of the thieves' three-vehicle caravan from Loomis Fargo to Reynolds & Reynolds, where Steve's other recruit, Eric, was waiting with a van rented earlier in the day from Budget. As the caravan neared Reynolds & Reynolds, where Eric was an employee, Steve called him on his cell phone. Eric had the gate open for them when they arrived.

Steve caught a glimpse of David before the redhead left with Kelly. Then, along with Eric and Scott, Steve began the next essential task of the heist—transferring mounds of loot from the Loomis Fargo van to the rented van. The plan then called for abandoning the Loomis van nearby in a secluded area.

Steve had recruited Scott Grant and Eric Payne into the theft with the promise of $100,000 for each. Scott had said he would get involved only if there were no guns. Eric demanded he not touch anything. Steve told them that there would be no guns and no need to leave fingerprints. And the job itself would be a piece of cake.

But periodic panic for the trio began right after David left with Kelly. Scott did not keep isolated the key David had placed in his hand, and now David was gone, and Scott had a key ring filled with about 125 keys, only one of which would open the Loomis van. Another equally large key ring in the front of the Loomis van was of equal use.

In the dark, Scott tried to insert one key into the slot. It didn't fit. Then another. It fit, but it wouldn't turn. Then another. Then another. Then still one more. Then another.

Steve cursed as Scott fumbled with the key ring. If they couldn't open the door, what would they do? The men were borderline hysterical, sweating in the cool October night. Maybe they would have to leave the money. Maybe a trail would lead the law to their homes. Or maybe they could bash the van's windows.

Ten frantic minutes later, after dozens of tries, Scott finally found the right key. But there was no time to celebrate. He quickly opened the back door.

The vision silenced them. Plastic bags of money in shrink-wrap filled the van almost top to bottom. Outside of the movies, they had never seen anything like it. Scott's and Eric's jaws dropped. They were in over their heads. This would change their lives.

"Unload it," Steve directed.

He told Eric to hop inside, but Eric refused, not wanting to touch the Loomis van, which could leave fingerprints. Remembering his agreement with Eric, Steve pushed his cousin toward the van. Once inside, Scott began passing stacks of cash out to Steve and Eric, who placed them in the rented van in blue plastic fifty-five-gallon barrels that Eric had swiped from the printing company's loading dock.

Scott's wish was for everyone to hurry up. As sweat moistened his face and clothes, he heard a siren in the night. Its wailing stunned the men as it grew louder and closer. Who could have tipped the police so soon? Scott walked to the edge of the Loomis van, felt himself stop breathing, put his hands up, and froze. He was ready to turn himself in.

The siren faded. They saw the flashing lights of an ambulance moving away from them in the dark on nearby Interstate 85. That was all it was, an ambulance. It seemed like either a cruel joke or a miracle. Relieved, they continued to move the bills.

Steve's cell phone rang. It was Kelly, passing an urgent reminder from David to make sure they took the two videotapes in the Loomis van. Steve reminded Scott to get them.

The men kept working, developing an easy rhythm as the minutes rolled by, taking armloads of cash from the Loomis van, walking a few yards to the Budget van, and filling the plastic barrels with money.

Then they ran out of room. The barrels lacked space for all the money, and they didn't want cash strewn around the van, in case a police officer stopped them on their not-so-innocent drive back to Steve's place.

Steve realized they would have to leave millions behind. Cool and in charge, he told Scott to ignore the stacks of ones and fives and stick to the larger denominations. As long as they had to leave some money, Steve hoped it would cloud the group's trail. Maybe whoever found it would steal it themselves.

The barrels were full about forty minutes after the money arrived at Reynolds & Reynolds. The next task was to abandon the white Loomis van. Scott and Steve handled this while Eric drove the rented van full of loot to a nearby British Petroleum filling station in Mount Holly, where the other two would meet him minutes later.

Followed by Steve's Mazda, Scott drove the Loomis van to a wooded area off Moores Chapel Road, about two-thirds of a mile from Reynolds & Reynolds. Forgetting to take the videotapes, Scott jumped out, closed the door, and hopped into Steve's car.

"Did you cut the van off?"

"No, I kept it running," Scott said.

Steve had wanted Scott to cut the van's engine. That way, if someone found the van loaded with gas, they might drive it away and so distract the FBI.

As they approached the BP station to meet Eric at about nine o'clock, Scott found yet another reason to sweat. A Mount Holly police car waited in the gas station's parking lot. The police officer had no clue anything was awry. And why would he? If he noticed them at all, it was as three young, mustachioed Southerners meeting at a convenience store. Still, Scott worried aloud to Steve, "We're gonna get caught."

Steve stayed cool. He never flinched in these situations. True, he had never done anything quite like this, but he had a solid career as a small-time crook under his belt. With the officer only dozens of feet from the Budget rental van, Steve maintained a nonchalant air, left the Mazda, and walked to the driver's seat of the loaded van. Scott slid behind the wheel of Steve's Mazda.

The police officer ignored them.

In two vehicles, the three men left the BP station and drove back on to I-85 and into the heart of Gaston County.

"I brought you into this because I trust you," Steve told Eric on the way. "If it went down, I know you wouldn't rat me out."

Steve called Scott on his cell phone to make sure his nervous cousin was all right. Scott said he was fine. The men exited Interstate 85 on to Route 321 North. That road started them on a thirty-minute ride into the northwest reaches of rural Lincoln County, to Steve's mobile home, which was located at the end of a gravel road, near a creek.

There, Steve's newly busty wife, Michele, waited with ten bags of rubber bands, a calculator, cardboard boxes, and a slashed-and-emptied mattress that one of her children had slept on in a bunk bed before it was gutted.

The men arrived. The money was theirs. It was time to count.

Steve and Eric carried the barrels into the mobile home while Scott looked for something to drink, to help him relax. He grabbed a Sun Drop soda. Eric was nervous, too.

Scott felt he had just made the worst mistake of his life. The twenty-six-year-old plant worker had dark hair and a medium build and spoke with one of the slower Southern drawls in rural Catawba County. He had obtained his GED at Gaston College two years earlier. He had a six-year-old daughter who lived with her mother. Scott lived with his girlfriend in a mobile home.

Eric stood five-foot-ten, weighed 190 pounds, and had a firm chin, a brown mustache, and a "Peace on Earth" tattoo. He looked tough, and he may not have been the nicest guy in the world, but he was not a major lawbreaker. The most serious conviction on his record was for driving while impaired. He and Steve had met as teenagers working at a sock factory in Belmont.

The loot counting began, assembly-line style. Scott passed bundles to Eric, who passed them to Steve, who called out the amounts written on the bundles to Michele, who added everything up on the calculator.

Nerves frayed. Eric paced the kitchen floor. Scott stopped counting when he reached $100,000. "We're gonna get caught," he kept saying. "We're gonna get caught."

"Calm down," Steve said. "We won't get caught if everyone does what they're supposed to do."

"We're gonna get caught," Scott said again, staring wide-eyed at the floor.

Michele, keeping tabs, just kept laughing. "Look at all this money! Look at all this money!"

Steve and Michele loaded twenty-dollar bills, in $10,000 stacks several inches thick, into the child's slashed mattress. They planned to close it up and put it back on the bunk bed.

Scott stopped pacing and leaned against the kitchen counter, folding his hands across his chest and staring at the mattress. "Jesus," he told Michele. "If that falls on your son's head, it's gonna kill him."

When the mattress was full of cash, Steve took one end and told Michele to grab the other. Together, they tried to lift it. It was too heavy. They unloaded the cash from the mattress back into the barrels.

Steve stayed calm throughout, swearing everybody in the group to eternal silence.

He again told Scott to be calm, just before his cousin left for the evening. The count had reached $2.7 million, and Scott couldn't bear to be around all that stolen money, though his nervousness didn't keep him from carrying $6,000 with him as his first installment. He would have taken more, but he didn't want to alert his girlfriend. Fearing he would be arrested, he managed to fall asleep next to her after returning home, only to be awakened by a loud pounding on the door and shouts of "Police! It's the police!" He tensed up. But it turned out to be just a drunken relative.

The others at Heist Central continued counting after Scott left, past midnight. Kelly, back from Columbia, joined them. The total was more than $14 million. Michele wrote it down on paper. "I'm rich," she said, laughing again. "I *love* this money!"

Steve paid Kelly and Eric almost $100,000 each—he would hold the rest of their shares—and Kelly drove Eric home.

Steve placed the money back in the barrels, covering the cash with dog food. Then he moved the barrels to a shed behind his mobile home and secured the shed with a Master Lock.

He went to sleep at six in the morning. When he woke up four hours later, he sent Michele to rent space at a storage facility about a mile from their home. Upon her return, he placed the barrels in the back of their Ford pickup truck, and together they drove to store the money. They locked their space securely and left.

The next day—Monday, October 6—Steve began taking the money back to his home. His cousin Nathan—who was Scott's brother—and Nathan's girlfriend, Amy, helped him move it to two facilities he felt were more secure, Bubba's Mini Storage and Lincoln Self Storage. Steve had arranged for Nathan Grant, a twenty-year-old mill worker, to rent space at these places, saying only that he needed to hide his gambling winnings. They put the money in duffel bags, cardboard boxes, and suitcases before stashing them. Bubba's Mini Storage and Lincoln Self Storage had vehicle-accessed gates that opened to security codes punched in by the driver. The storage lockers themselves were secured by keys, which only Nathan and Steve kept.

For their help, Steve would pay Nathan and Amy $70,000. The circle of heist beneficiaries was widening.

Earlier that day, October 6, Michele Chambers, holding a black briefcase filled with cash, had walked into a NationsBank branch office in Mount Holly, about six miles west of the scene of the crime. She had approached the teller, a woman with glasses.

Michele had a high voice she could make sound mature. "How much cash can I deposit without you having to file paperwork?" she asked the teller.

The teller told her $10,000, in accordance with a federal law about mandatory bank reports for large cash deposits. The teller did not say so, but the purpose of the reports was to alert authorities to possible money laundering.

Michele opened her briefcase on the ledge beneath the teller's window, reached into it, and lifted out bands of twenty-dollar bills totaling $9,500.

The teller kept her eyes steady, saying nothing out of the ordinary. But Michele, sensing the teller thought her crazy, felt a need to reassure. "Don't worry," Michele said. "It's not drug money."

The teller accepted the bundles, and Michele left.

Once outside, she hopped into the waiting Mazda 626 with her husband, Steve, who was in the driver's seat. They did not see the teller, inside the bank, fill out a Suspicious Activity Report. That's the form filed with federal authorities when a bank is suspicious about a cash transaction, even one less than $10,000. Her paperwork, though, would not reach area law enforcement for about three months, after it had passed through official channels. But on this day, less than forty-eight hours after the crime, one of the banks that rightfully owned some of the stolen money had $9,500 of it back.

Steve and Michele did not plan to live in their mobile home much longer. They were going to break the spending rules of the group, rules they never intended to follow because Steve thought the FBI would not be able to connect him to David Ghantt.

They had begun searching for a luxury house a few weeks before the heist, signing up with a real-estate agent. Looking at homes priced $200,000 and higher, they had settled on a seven-thousand-square-foot beauty with a curved staircase, a stucco exterior, and a price tag of $635,000. It was high on a small mountain in Gaston County, North Carolina, where Steve and Michele had grown up.

On October 5, the day after the theft, Steve and Michele signed an offer to buy it and set a closing date for later in the month. They agreed to pay $10,000 up front as good-faith money, $400,000 in cash, and $225,000 in financed payments. The prospect of moving excited Steve and Michele, who had been a couple for about five years.

Michele, a former office manager at Nationwide Insurance in Belmont, North Carolina, went by the nickname "Shelley." An attractive woman and a snazzy dresser, she had beautiful breasts that she was not shy to show people, because they were only ten months old. She had bought them for about $2,000 apiece in December 1996, as a Christmas present to herself.

She grew up just outside the small town of Mount Holly in Gaston

Most of David Ghantt's accomplices took the bulk of the stolen cash to this mobile home in Lincoln County, North Carolina, in which Steve and Michele Chambers lived until three weeks after the heist.
Robert Lahser / CHARLOTTE OBSERVER

County. Though her parents divorced when she was a child, Michele's life was mostly calm until she was thirteen years old. That's when she and her mom, Sandra Floyd, fell into a bitter argument over Michele's not coming straight home from cheerleading practice one day. Sandra told Michele she could not be a cheerleader. Michele told her mom she was moving out.

She moved in with her father, Benny Loftin. But Benny and Michele had trouble, too. At age nineteen, she married Norman Harris, a working-class man who would join the marines after they had a child together. They later had a second child. Michele wanted children at a young age because she had learned that she would soon need a partial hysterectomy because of a health condition.

Before Norman Harris joined the armed forces and left Michele to fend for herself with a child and a job that failed to pay all the bills, he innocently introduced her to Steve Chambers, who at the time was dating Norman's sister, Angel. Steve and Michele did not get along, especially when Steve took sides with Norman in arguments between the couple.

He was a fast talker, this Steve Chambers. He had a brown goatee and a six-foot-one, 220-pound build that straddled the line between stocky and fat. He, too, had worked low-paying jobs. But he had come to see a more promising future in loansharking and bookmaking.

His friends knew him to be fascinated by the Northeastern mob culture, at least as he had seen it portrayed in Hollywood, in the *Godfather* movies and *Goodfellas*. He used lines, with friends, like "Don't tell nobody nothin' " and "Keep your mouth shut"—not to spoof Robert De Niro, but as part of his own style. He took his friends to eat at Godfather's Pizza. He flashed phony IDs.

His friends did not know that Steve had an unusual relationship with the FBI as an informant for crimes that didn't happen—crimes that he himself had discussed performing alongside the duped friends he was informing on. He had informed on his friend Mike McKinney in that manner. Mike had helped Steve in a drunken, failed attempt to rob an ATM, and Steve told the feds they should investigate him. He once revealed supposed plans for an armored-car robbery that never materialized. Steve even had a favorite agent, Phil King. He would call and ask King how much money he would receive for information that would solve a specific crime. Steve didn't know that the FBI had written him off as an informant.

From a young age, Steve had associated with people with criminal histories. He dropped out of East Gaston High School before finishing the tenth grade. Then he drove a truck for a while, worked for Coca-Cola, and pulled off some low-level crimes with friends.

When Norman Harris asked Steve to look after Michele while he was away in the marines, Steve took the request seriously. Too seriously. He spent time with Michele and her children, bringing food to their apartment and helping them get by. He would hug and kiss the kids, read to them, and take them places. His caring did not go unnoticed by their mother, who, one day as Steve was about to leave, told him she loved him. He told Michele he loved her, too, and they kissed.

Michele and her mother had repaired their relationship by then. But, Michele's mother was not pleased with her daughter's infidelity. That's why Steve Chambers and Sandra Floyd did not get along. But there was nothing she could do, and Steve and Michele married in November 1996.

At her second wedding, Michele wore an A-cup bra under a traditional white dress. But she had always had ambitions for her breasts, even as a child, when she would walk into lingerie stores to try on bras and see what size she wanted. A 34-C had long been her goal. In December 1996, nine months after her wedding to Steve, she accomplished her goal. Steve opposed the surgery, fearing it would hurt her.

Besides stashing the money in Bubba's Mini Storage and Lincoln

Self Storage, Steve kept some around his home. He buried about $150,000 in a duffel bag, in a hole off a trail near the creek behind his mobile home.

Steve's next bit of heist business was 530 miles away. Since he did not like flying, he traveled by car. The week after the theft, he and Eric Payne drove to a motel in Evansville, Indiana, to pay Mike McKinney $50,000. McKinney, who worked construction, received the fee for having given Steve his birth certificate and social security card, which David Ghantt had used for his fake ID. McKinney did not know the truth about what his IDs were being used for. Steve told him that a friend needed them to leave the country because he had shot someone.

Just after the theft, Steve had wired $2,000 of heist money to McKinney to help him pay a fine for driving while intoxicated. Steve had known McKinney for about four years, having met him when McKinney was on leave from the marines with Norman Harris, who took him to Gastonia. McKinney had served in Okinawa, Somalia, and Camp Lejeune, North Carolina.

On this day, October 15, 1997, Steve had a suitcase packed with $50,000 in plastic-wrapped $10 bills. He opened it at the motel, took the cash out, and counted it.

Eric asked McKinney, "Do you know where this came from?"

Steve told Eric to be quiet. He told McKinney that somebody else had stolen the money from the Mafia. Then he took McKinney aside. "There's a guy who needs to be taken out," Steve said quietly. "Do you want it?"

The marines had booted McKinney after his urine tested positive for cocaine, but he still knew how to use a gun. Steve hoped he would fly to Mexico and shoot David dead. He didn't tell McKinney that the target was the man using McKinney's ID. He simply said he would pay him $250,000 in cash.

McKinney said he would do it.

Steve said he would get in touch with him about it later.

Killing David Ghantt would eliminate the heist's top suspect, and with him the possibility that he could ever lead the FBI to Kelly and Steve. Plus, they could split his heist share.

Meanwhile, Steve kept in contact with Michele at home, on his cell phone. One night, she told him it was raining hard outside. Steve worried about the $150,000 he had buried behind the mobile home. He told Michele she needed to unearth it before it got soaked and was worthless. Michele did not know where the duffel bag was buried. Steve had not marked the site, for obvious reasons. He gave her painstaking directions over the phone.

Michele was wearing a T-shirt and jeans. It was pouring, and it was dark. She heard thunder and saw occasional streaks of lightning. But Steve had told her to get the money, so she hurried, trotting outside with her head down, so rain would not get in her eyes.

Terrified, she fell to her knees and dug with her hands. She couldn't find the money. Rain dripped from her hair, mixing with the tears in her eyes and running down her cheeks. She was outside for twenty minutes, but the rain did not stop. She was a weeping wreck.

Finally, she gave up. Steve would have to find the money himself.

He arrived two days later. Quickly locating the duffel bag, he found that the twenty-dollar bills inside it were stuck together in green gobs.

The situation called for some innovative money laundering. They placed the gobs into their laundry dryer. Michele clicked the machine to the delicate cycle. Before they turned it on, Steve suggested they throw poker chips in with the "wash," saying he had once heard their presence would help keep bills apart. The technique had been used by a counterfeiter in the movie *To Live and Die in L.A.*

They waited near the machine as the money flipped around inside. It worked. The money was still good. And it was warm—warm enough to roll around naked in. Which they didn't do.

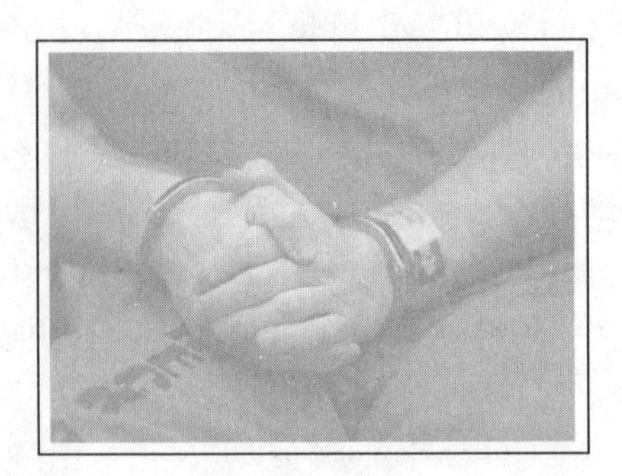

How Baseball Hindered the FBI

DAVID GHANTT probably didn't know it was there.

That was the speculation of three FBI agents and the Loomis Fargo manager. They were watching, the morning after the heist, the security tape that had not been swiped. Why else would Ghantt have stolen only two tapes when there were three? The one that remained had been locked in a cabinet in the manager's office, unlike the others, which had been in plain view.

FBI agents Dick Womble, Mark Rozzi, and Rick Schwein sat in the Loomis manager's office staring at a TV screen just before noon on October 5. Watching video of the previous night, the Loomis manager was furious. Ghantt had almost been fired earlier in the week for leaving money unattended, briefly, outside the city's Federal Reserve building. Was this revenge for his getting yelled at? To make matters worse, the stolen money was not marked with known serial numbers.

Womble, Rozzi, and Schwein, immersed in their investigative task, were pleased that Ghantt had left one tape behind. They did not mind that the video quality was mediocre—black-and-white and not terribly clear. After many robberies, FBI agents and detectives learn that stricken companies have not replaced security tapes for a long time and that the videos are worthless. But this one left no doubt that Ghantt was the thief. His thin frame and thinning hair were easily identifiable. A prosecutor armed with this tape would waltz through an open-and-shut court case.

Womble was excited there was a clear suspect, though no one knew yet how much money was missing. Loomis workers were not able to open the vault because Ghantt had maliciously set the security timer and had taken both sets of keys.

Watching the video was not like watching a movie. It recorded the views from sixteen cameras, one at a time, for a second or two before switching to a different view. In some angles, viewers saw only an arm, a leg, or nothing at all.

"It's amazing how much time he took," Womble said.

The other agents watching agreed. Ghantt started around 6:45 P.M. and didn't finish for about an hour.

They also were astonished by the amount of work involved in moving what seemed like more than a ton of cash. Even a stronger man than Ghantt would have had trouble with that amount. The agents watched the entire video, some of it in fast-forward mode, and they saw nobody besides Ghantt. It seemed like he did it himself.

The FBI had been working the case since that morning. Loomis officials had called the Charlotte-Mecklenburg Police about nine-thirty on October 5, after their employees had been unable to enter the vault. The police then called the FBI, because most of the money Loomis Fargo hauled around belonged to banks, and bank robberies are federal crimes. Schwein, the on-duty agent that weekend, fielded the police call and immediately notified the bureau's violent crime investigators—known in Charlotte's FBI office as Squad Six. Squad Six, which included Womble and Rozzi, regularly investigated bank thefts, even nonviolent ones. Charlotte's FBI had recently helped recover the money stolen by Philip Noel Johnson, who had hidden most of his $18.8 million Loomis stash in a shed in the mountains of western North Carolina.

In talking to the Loomis warehouse manager, Womble, Rozzi, and Schwein learned that the firm had first suspected three employees it could not contact. But one turned up in church, and another also had been located. The only one still missing was Ghantt. He had worked at the warehouse the previous night with a trainee and nobody else, Loomis officials told the FBI. A twenty-seven-year-old vault supervisor, Ghantt had no criminal record. But Loomis officials shared that he had almost been fired for the Federal Reserve incident.

The warehouse alarm had actually gone off the night before, because Ghantt had incorrectly programmed it after stealing the money. But the police had arrived and departed uneventfully after checking the building's exterior and noticing nothing askew.

If it was true that more than $10 million had been stolen, as Loomis officials believed, it was one of the biggest heists in United States history. The FBI needed to know, quickly, as much as possible about David Ghantt, in order to find him.

The Federal Bureau of Investigation, founded in 1908, has taken advantage of many of the world's technological advances. But the first part of most investigations still involves basic person-to-person interviews. Besides providing useful information, a good interview can develop into two or three more interviews, each of which can lead to tips that provide even more information.

Agent Womble was in charge of interviewing Ghantt's relatives. He quickly learned that Ghantt's wife, sisters, and parents were as shocked as the Loomis officials. David's wife, Tammy, said she was clueless about everything. She was also terrified that her husband was missing. Womble believed her on both counts.

That did not mean she lacked value to the FBI. Womble learned from Tammy and her in-laws that Ghantt was born October 20, 1969, in Gastonia, North Carolina. David had been married to Tammy for five years. They had no children. They lived in a mobile home.

Tammy refused to believe her husband was a calculating thief. David was caring, nice, sweet, gentle, and funny, Tammy told Womble. Somebody must have put him up to it, she believed. "This is not my David," Tammy said.

Last night had started as a normal one for her, Womble learned. She ate with her mom at the Cracker Barrel restaurant in Gastonia. She called David at Loomis Fargo and told him not to grab dinner on the way home. She had takeout for him—chicken and potatoes.

"Refrigerate it," David had told her. "I'll be home late tonight."

Late meant eight or nine o'clock, Tammy figured. So she worried when she awoke at one in the morning and was alone under the covers in their mobile home forty minutes west of Charlotte in the city of Kings Mountain. She called David at work, then on his pager, then on his cell phone, then on his pager again. Nothing. She had always been nervous he might catch a bullet working for Loomis Fargo, with all that money around. It was a dangerous job.

Finally, at two-thirty, she telephoned David's parents in Hendersonville, nearly two hours west in the North Carolina mountains. She told them their son was missing, and they said they would rush over. Then Tammy called the Charlotte-Mecklenburg Police. An officer told her they couldn't do anything because David lived in Kings Mountain, located in Cleveland County. So Tammy called the Cleveland County Sheriff's Office. They said *they* couldn't do anything because David had last been seen in Charlotte. Finally, Tammy talked to a Charlotte-Mecklenburg police officer who promised to investigate. When she hung up, she paced the mobile home's floor and stared at the wall, where framed pictures of David stared back.

At about five o'clock, David's parents arrived in Kings Mountain, haggard from worry and lack of sleep. The three spent the rest of the night discussing what to do. First thing in the morning, they decided, they would put up missing-person posters of David in Gastonia and Charlotte. Maybe they would look for a private eye, since the cops struck them as reluctant to help.

Then, in the morning, the authorities called to say they had found David's pickup truck in the Loomis parking lot.

In the early afternoon, agent Rozzi called to ask if Tammy could come to Charlotte's FBI office to talk.

Where was David? Was he hurt? Was he dead? Tammy was desperate to know, but Rozzi had no answers.

At four o'clock in the afternoon, agents John Wydra and Julia Mueller were dispatched to the Loomis warehouse to help other FBI agents with crime-scene work. They examined the building's interior, dusted for fingerprints, and searched Ghantt's abandoned pickup truck.

They started interviewing current and former Loomis Fargo employees for what they knew about the heist and about Ghantt. They quickly learned that Ghantt had few close friends and that nobody from work seemed to know him very well. Wydra and Mueller talked to about twenty Loomis workers, gaining a few tidbits here and there but nothing that revealed a clear path to Ghantt's whereabouts. Their interviews were easy, not accusatory, but they watched for signals that the employees were lying. Nothing seemed clear, though they took down a few names of other people who maybe knew more.

Wydra usually worked for the Charlotte FBI branch's Squad Four, focusing on white-collar crime. His specialty was tracing money laundering. But on this day, almost all the agents were working with Squad Six, the violent crime unit. Wydra's Squad Four work would be delayed for a while as he, Womble, Rozzi, and the others tried to sort out the basic mysteries. Was David Ghantt dead? If he was alive, where did he go? Did he take the money with him? Did he leave any clues? And how the hell did he pull this off, anyway? Did someone help him?

Early that evening, the agents and their supervisors assembled in downtown Charlotte's Wachovia Building, the eighth, ninth, and tenth floors of which made up the FBI's headquarters for North Carolina. It was becoming apparent that almost all of Charlotte's FBI agents would be asked to work this case almost exclusively for several days, maybe weeks.

On the ninth floor, around the Squad Six desks and cubicles, Womble and Rozzi briefed the others on what they had learned about the main suspect from his relatives. They also mentioned that Ghantt earned just over eight dollars an hour.

The other agents shook their heads in quiet amazement at Ghantt's daring. The man just took the money and ran. The agents also were amazed to learn that even now, Loomis Fargo could not open the vault to count its losses. The company planned to break into the vault the next day. Short of dynamite, there was nothing it could do to get inside before then. Company officials had an idea how much was missing—about $15 million—but they were not certain. There was only one rock-solid piece of information, compliments of the videotape.

Given the approximate amount stolen, the agents realized that solving this case would be quite a coup for Charlotte's FBI office. They also realized that not solving it could be embarrassing, given David Ghantt's inexperience as a criminal.

Some in the FBI wondered if Ghantt had been shot by a co-conspirator just after the theft, but federal prosecutors assumed he was still alive. On Sunday afternoon, agents contacted the on-call weekend prosecutor, a man named David Keesler. The following day, Keesler had Womble read the evidence against Ghantt to a federal grand jury that happened to have its regularly scheduled monthly meeting in Charlotte that day.

Womble told the jurors about the work schedule that had left David at the Loomis warehouse Saturday night, about the company videotape, and about the missing Loomis van. It was an open-and-shut indictment. By day's end, David Ghantt was charged with bank larceny.

For that, the maximum penalty was ten years in prison and a fine. All the agents had to do was find him.

At about 5:40 P.M., soon after Womble completed his testimony to the grand jury, the FBI received a phone call from a man who had just finished mowing his lawn in western Mecklenburg County. The man had noticed a seemingly abandoned white vehicle in the woods and said it fit the description of the missing Loomis van broadcast on the news.

The tip pumped up everyone in Charlotte's FBI office. Maybe the van had all the missing money. Maybe David was inside, handcuffed. Or, some speculated, maybe David was inside dead.

About six agents and Loomis officials arrived at the wooded area, a lovers' lane littered with beer cans and cigarette butts, late in the

David Ghantt loaded the $17 million into this van on October 4, 1997. His accomplices unloaded all but $3.3 million. An informant saw the abandoned van in the woods two days later and called the FBI.
Stephanie Grace Lim / CHARLOTTE OBSERVER

afternoon. Immediately, they saw it was the right truck.

The doors were locked, so they looked in the tinted windows. Inside, they saw mounds of money, still shrink-wrapped, behind the driver's seat. It was clear to the Loomis officials that most of the stolen money was not there. It was not clear if there was a body under the money.

They called a flatbed truck to haul the Loomis van to an FBI garage at headquarters, where they could examine its contents in a secure area. There, with FBI supervisor Vic O'Korn present, they opened the vehicle and quickly noticed that the stacks of bills were mostly ones and fives. It seemed the thieves had taken the larger denominations. On the front seat were David Ghantt's gun and the two other Loomis surveillance videotapes that had been stolen. Why would he have left them behind?

Counting the money took only half an hour, as the wrappers around the stacks were marked with their totals: $3.3 million altogether, less than one-fifth of the amount missing. The FBI knew this because Loomis had used heavy machinery to break through the vault's steel-and-concrete wall earlier in the day to discover the amount of cash stolen: $17,044,033.

Mileage records for the van showed it had not been driven far after the heist. The value of that information seemed minimal, given that the money was obviously off-loaded. Maybe David had rented a vehicle nearby.

FBI supervisors dispatched agents to show Ghantt's picture at rental-car companies in town. But none of the clerks recognized his face.

The command post for Charlotte's FBI, on the tenth floor of the Wachovia Building, was packed with desks and computers. It was used mainly when agents gathered to work on and discuss major crimes. During non-crisis times, the walls contained a Charlotte street map, a North Carolina state map, a map of the world, and a map of

Charlotte/Douglas International Airport. On this day, the walls had aerial pictures of the Loomis Fargo warehouse, a picture of David Ghantt's mobile home, a picture of the white Loomis van, and the phone numbers of Ghantt and his relatives. A larger conference room would host twice-daily briefings, at seven in the morning and five in the afternoon.

This evening, the predominant opinion at headquarters was that David Ghantt likely had accomplices. It seemed improbable he could have pulled this off alone. Under a solo scenario, he probably would have had to plant a second vehicle in the secluded area where the Loomis van was found, then transfer the money by himself from the Loomis van to the second vehicle, and then drive the second vehicle away. Even at that, he presumably would have needed a ride from someone after planting the second vehicle in the first place.

Then there was the money left behind. If Ghantt had acted alone, he probably would have made proper accommodations for all the money he stole. Maybe, this theory continued, he had accomplices whose vehicle was just too small to fit everything. On a simpler level, the amount of money stolen—more than a ton, at 2,748 pounds and sixty-four cubic feet of bills—was likely too heavy a load for such a skinny guy. That he had moved it once, from the vault to the Loomis van, was impressive enough, but the prospect of his transferring it all into another vehicle by himself seemed unlikely. In either case, the FBI noted the thief's or thieves' presence of mind in focusing on the large bills. The mounds of recovered cash comprised, in total, two-fifths of the weight of all the money stolen, even though they constituted only one-fifth the amount.

The week after the theft, agents Wydra and Mueller interviewed dozens of past and current Loomis Fargo employees. A few told them Ghantt had recently said he was dating a former worker there. The name of this alleged girlfriend was Kelly Jane Campbell, and everyone said she was blunt and full of attitude. She had stopped working at Loomis about a year earlier.

The dominant early impression the agents had of Ghantt was that of a loner, so if his colleagues were mentioning this Campbell woman, maybe she knew something. They decided to check her out. Wydra and Mueller kept interviewing Loomis employees while two other agents drove to Kelly Campbell's home on Tuesday.

The route took agents Gerry Senatore and David Martinez from Charlotte's urban streets of bank and office buildings to the back roads of rural Gaston County. The agents turned off a two-lane road on to a gravel street that looked like it dead-ended into tall trees but actually kept going through the trees into hidden, winding asphalt roads that passed a compound of mobile homes unseen from the main street. At the end of the road—which, coincidentally, was named Kelly Road—Kelly Campbell lived in a white mobile home surrounded by the goats, dogs, and roosters kept by her and her husband, Jimmy, nicknamed "Spanky."

The agents knocked on her door. She opened it. They said they were with the FBI.

Kelly Campbell was tall and pleasantly plump and had dirty-blond shoulder-length hair. She did not smile often, even around people she could tolerate. When she did smile, her broad-featured face turned cute, her eyes shiny and her grin sweet.

She was not smiling now. Her daughter was there, and Kelly called her father, who lived nearby, to come pick up the girl for a while. Then the agents sat down in her living room and told her about the theft and about David Ghantt. They told her that people at Loomis Fargo said they had dated. Did she know anything?

Kelly Campbell said she had heard about the heist but that she didn't know anything. She and David were friends, she said, but they had not dated. She described Ghantt as quick tempered and goofy and said they had smoked some pot together, but that was it.

The agents didn't care about her pot smoking, but they wanted to see if she was telling the truth. They asked if she had any marijuana at home.

She said she did.

One agent asked her to bring it to them.

"Why?" Campbell asked. "So you and your buddy can go down the road and smoke it?"

She brought out about an ounce. The other Loomis employees were right, the agents thought; Kelly Campbell was blunt.

They asked if she had any idea where Ghantt was.

She said he liked the mountains and maybe was staying around Hendersonville or Wilkesboro, North Carolina, where his parents lived.

They asked if she would take a lie-detector test.

She declined.

The agents were persistent, but they realized her reluctance might center around the drugs or a possible affair with David. Besides, they could tell she was not exactly living the high life.

They decided they would keep an eye on her. Just in case.

"Van, Driver, Money Missing," read the lead headline on the front page of the October 6, 1997, *Charlotte Observer*, the biggest newspaper in the Carolinas. "A very substantial amount of money," possibly as much as $15 million, had vanished, along with an armored car and the driver, David Ghantt, the story said. It continued, "If the money was stolen and that amount is correct, this would be one of the largest heists in U.S. history. The same company, Loomis, Fargo & Co., lost $18.83 million in March in a heist in Jacksonville, Fla."

Ghantt, according to the newspaper and the TV news on Monday, was six-foot-one and had strawberry blond hair and blue eyes. He weighed about 165 pounds. He had a tattoo of a pistol and a rose on his left arm, the FBI said. This was a mistake; actually, Ghantt had a Lynyrd Skynyrd tattoo.

The media planned to closely monitor developments in the investigation. Shortly after the story appeared, *Observer* editors dispatched two reporters to David Ghantt's mobile home in Kings Mountain. Their task was to prompt his relatives to tell the newspaper more about him. They parked a few homes away from Ghantt's and knocked on his door. A man answered and promptly—though politely—asked them to leave. Tammy and the rest of David's relatives were too upset to talk with the press.

The newspaper also sent reporters to search public records to learn about Ghantt. They obtained a copy of Ghantt's marriage certificate from the Gaston County Courthouse and a copy of his gun permit from the Cleveland County Courthouse. They called the records department of the United States Army for information on his military service. They also fielded calls from his local and military friends. It was all basic biographical material, so the newspaper could paint a picture of David Ghantt. And that was the gist of the coverage—basic

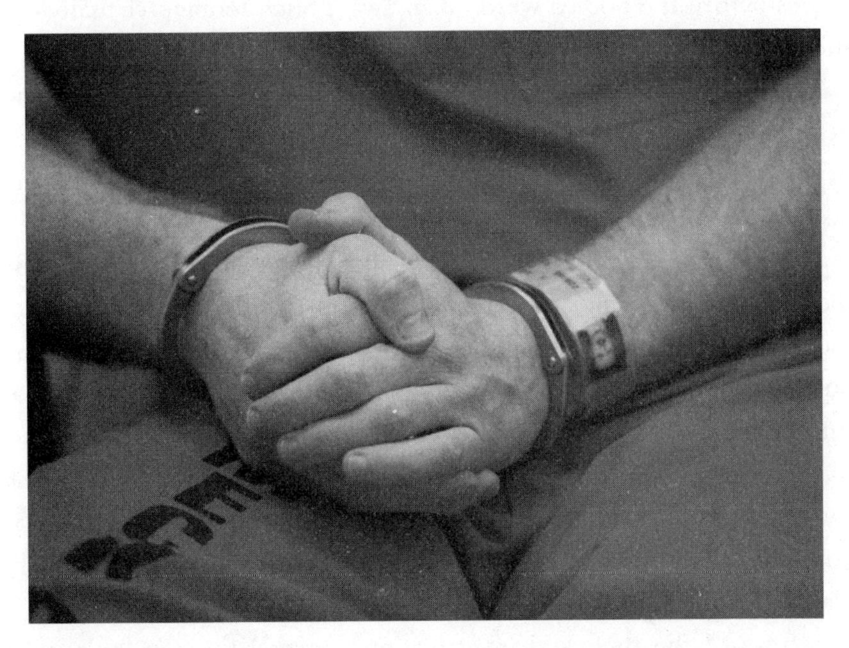

The FBI interviewed friends and relatives of David Ghantt in the days after the theft.
CHARLOTTE OBSERVER

information about a man who seemed basic, except for his recent act. Reporters suspected that if he was alive, he was far away, though some suggested that anybody who would steal so much cash might be stupid enough to stick around the scene of the crime.

Gary German hoped David Ghantt was nearby, just because it would be funnier that way. Gary was not a reporter. Rather, he was one of the strangest steady newspaper sources the *Observer* had ever had. He was a talkative, foul-mouthed man who was permanently bedridden from a car accident and who did little with his time but listen to police scanners so he could hear officers' radio transmissions. Fascinated by local crime, he took it upon himself to alert newspapers and TV stations to nighttime street trouble that slipped beneath their radar. Local media did not fully staff their newsrooms twenty-four hours a day, but night-owl Gary knew about crime when it happened, and his early-morning calls to TV camera people helped them reach crime scenes before the bodies were taken away. Such footage virtually ensured that a story made the TV news.

Gary lived off Gaston County crime, getting monthly checks from newspapers and TV stations for his calls. He claimed that he gave booze to select local law-enforcement officers in exchange for news tips, and he called reporters at home in the middle of the night when he deemed the events of the streets newsworthy. During the day, he would phone the newspapers' crime reporters in Gaston County and tell them of the most recent incidents, not even bothering to say hello but starting out with the likes of, "Got yourself a shootin' on Airline Avenue. That sumbitch emptied his bullets and got his ass *outta* there."

Gary's law-enforcement friends did not include FBI agents, so he had nothing of value to share with the media on the heist. The FBI was not telling the press about Kelly Campbell, revealing only that it thought David Ghantt might have had help.

News of the theft and investigation adorned the *Observer*'s front page the Monday, Tuesday, and Wednesday after the heist, but on Thursday, October 9, Dean Smith, the revered basketball coach of the University of North Carolina, announced his retirement, knocking the heist news to the Local section.

During the first weeks after the heist, the agents worked sixteen-hour days. Womble stayed in touch with Tammy Ghantt and David's other relatives, trying to reconstruct David's forty-eight hours prior to the theft. The agents learned little of value except that David was an avid reader of detective novels. All that meant for the FBI was that he may have considered their investigative techniques and had probably been thinking about the crime for a while.

Womble, Rozzi, and other agents took posters of Ghantt around town, hoping someone would spot him and call the authorities. On their own, people were calling the FBI with supposed sightings of Ghantt at the airport or at a topless bar—leads that wound up nowhere. The agents took pictures of Ghantt to those places and showed them to people there. They also drove to hotels to check registration books and show his picture to clerks, just in case he had used a phony name to check in. John Wydra and other agents interviewed workers at businesses near the Loomis Fargo building, on Wilkinson Boulevard, to see if anybody had heard or seen anything unusual the night of the theft. The only clue came from the manager at Niko's sandwich shop, who said Ghantt had eaten lunch there hours before the theft. The information was appreciated but offered no valuable help.

Also of little use were the FBI's efforts at dozens of area inns. A NASCAR race the weekend of the heist had drawn thousands, complicating agents' efforts to check if anybody matched Ghantt's description. Many who did look similar to Ghantt had themselves been staying under assumed names at their motels. Tracking them down turned out to be a waste of time.

About a week into the investigation, information presented in the twice-daily FBI briefings yielded another clue that Ghantt had help, and that a woman was probably involved. The clue came from Ghantt's pager, from the numbers entered before and during the theft. His pager records showed that most of the calls had come from his own cell phone number. Certainly, he did not call it himself, the FBI figured. It had to be someone else using Ghantt's cell phone, which seemed a clever attempt to keep the feds off the accomplice's trail.

But one number sequence repeated often in the pager seemed intriguing: 143, 143, 143. At first, the agents—most of them in their thirties and forties—had no idea what it meant. Womble and Wydra were sitting in the command post when another agent said he remembered reading about 143 messages in a recent newspaper story about beeper-speak. It meant "I love you," because *I* has one letter, *love* has four, and *you* has three. The recollection spurred another agent, Phil King, to remember that his daughter's boyfriend often punched 143 into her pager.

The FBI did not know who had entered the code, but the numbers were a sign that a woman besides his wife probably communicated with Ghantt during the theft.

With the first week after the heist mostly a bust, a basic crime-fighting mantra stared Charlotte's forty FBI agents square in the face: As time passes, the chance of solving a crime decreases. Unexpected things happen. Evidence disappears. Potential witnesses leave town or die or forget faces, names, and dates.

On October 11, exactly one week after the heist, most of the agents gathered in the command post to watch the TV show *America's Most Wanted*, scheduled to air a segment on Ghantt across the country that night at nine o'clock on the East Coast. Other agents positioned themselves on the city's streets so they could quickly check the flood of tips they expected would barrage the office after the show. Meanwhile, these agents canvassed every business located on the most direct route from the Loomis Fargo warehouse to where the van was found in the woods. They asked if anyone had seen anything suspicious on October 4. Nobody had.

The bulk of the staff ate pizza for dinner and waited for the show, whose producers often worked with the FBI. First broadcast in 1988, the show was credited with helping catch hundreds of criminals. Wydra, Rozzi, supervisor Rick Shaffer, and others watched a baseball game on the TV in the command post, a playoff game between the Cleveland Indians and the Baltimore Orioles. *America's Most Wanted* was scheduled on the same channel directly after the game.

At first, the room was filled with excitement and anticipation over potential new tips. But not for long. The score of the game—initially a concern only to the Indians and Orioles fans among the agents—soon worried everyone. That's because as nine o'clock approached, the game was tied and in extra innings. If neither team scored immediately, the game would probably preempt the Ghantt segment of the show. Or maybe not, the agents hoped. Maybe the network would air all of the show anyway. The agents did not know.

To the dismay of everyone, the game did not end until almost 10:00 P.M., when the Indians' Marquis Grissom crossed home plate in the twelfth inning, four hours and fifty-one minutes after the game began. That made it the longest League Championship Series game in baseball history.

The agents quickly saw that the station would indeed air *America's Most Wanted* after the game, but not from the beginning. Details of another crime were being shown when it came on. Then a commercial filled the screen. Maybe the Ghantt segment would be next, they hoped.

When the show came back on, the narrator told viewers to call the show if they saw David Ghantt. That meant the Ghantt segment was already over, without anybody on the East Coast having seen it. Epithets filled the room. Agents fired wadded paper and crumpled Doritos bags at the screen. Supervisor Shaffer, an Indians fan, held his head in his hands. Wydra and the others sat stunned. Only people in the Western time zones saw the Ghantt segment that night.

The agents positioned on the street learned nothing valuable. The FBI received one Ghantt tip that evening. A West Coast caller said he thought he had seen Ghantt gambling at a casino in Las Vegas. The caller was not sure which one. It was barely worth following.

The FBI believed David Ghantt's wife, Tammy, when she said the day after the crime that she knew nothing about the heist. And surveillance of her had turned up nothing. She even helped them tape the *America's Most Wanted* segment, ending it by pleading to her husband, "Please, if there's any way possible, call us or the FBI and let us know you are alive and well. . . . And remember, David, no matter what, we do love you."

Agents gave her a lie-detector test anyway, to be on the safe side. Though the results of lie-detector tests are not considered reliable enough to be allowed as evidence at trials, many agents, detectives, and prosecutors find them solid enough for use in investigations.

Agent Bob Drdak conducted the test, asking an emotionally shriveled Tammy basic questions.

Had she seen David since the theft?

She said she hadn't.

Had she talked to him since?

Again, she said she hadn't.

The test results came back inconclusive, which was a surprise to the agents, who had felt beforehand that she would easily pass.

Two days later, on October 13, she was tested again. But first, Drdak asked Tammy if she had doubted any of her answers two days earlier.

She replied that when he asked if she had seen David, she thought of his picture near the foot of her bed. She had seen the picture, as well as their home videos, which was like seeing him, she had thought. So maybe she hadn't answered that question with certainty. The same was true when he asked if she had talked to David. Since the theft, she had called his voice mail and heard his voice.

Drdak explained that he was interested only in whether she had actually seen him alive, or heard him speak to her live. He then rephrased his polygraph questions accordingly.

"Besides seeing his picture in your bedroom or on home videos, have you seen David since the theft?"

"No," Tammy said.

"Besides on voice mail, have you heard his voice since the theft?"

"No," she said.

Tammy passed the polygraph test.

High Times, Home and Abroad

KELLY CAMPBELL WAS NERVOUS and scared. And when Kelly Campbell was nervous and scared, Kelly Campbell smoked pot. Lots of pot.

In the two weeks after the heist, Kelly, twenty-seven, smoked marijuana morning, afternoon, and night. And she had solid reason to be nervous and scared. She had lied point-blank to the FBI when the agents came to her door. She had been in contact with David, having received a page when he arrived in Mexico. She knew she would fail an FBI lie-detector test.

After the agents left, she had called Steve Chambers for advice. He told her not to worry about it. He had a lawyer for her to call. The lawyer would call the FBI.

Steve told Kelly that the Loomis loot was hidden "up north" with three men he knew who ran a crooked bank that was charging them a fee. He had a lawyer because the local police had recently arrested him in an unrelated case, before the heist, for writing $30,000 in fraudulent checks. His lawyer, a short, salt-and-pepper-haired man named Jeff Guller, was negotiating a plea bargain for Steve that could keep him out of jail. Steve would have to plead guilty to forty-two counts of obtaining property by false pretenses, a felony.

Guller, the lawyer, met with Kelly. She told him she did not want to take a lie-detector test. Guller did not press her for information. He took the business card the agents had given her, called the FBI, and left a voice-mail message that he represented Kelly Campbell and that she did not want to take a polygraph.

Kelly and Steve had grown up together, their friendship formed at teenage outdoor drinking parties on the back roads of Gaston County. They lost touch after high school until the mid-1990s, when Steve contacted Kelly with a scam in mind. He wanted to pay her for her husband's employee number on his W-2 tax form, which Steve would use to file a phony tax return. She obliged.

She and Steve began hanging out. In late 1996, Kelly found herself outside Steve's home, listening to music with a bunch of Steve's friends, grilling steaks, drinking, and playing cards. She had recently quit her Loomis Fargo job. Steve verbally cornered her. How many people worked on an armored truck? When was the best time of day to knock one off? Did she know anyone who might team up with them for an inside job?

And so it was that momentum for the second-largest heist in United States history originated over Budweiser and Uno outside a mobile home in rural North Carolina.

Steve had pondered a heist of his own for years—it just seemed like it could be done, he thought. But on that day, Kelly said, "Don't even think about it, Steve. It's too dangerous. Armored-car drivers carry guns."

Steve was persistent. Maybe, he suggested, they could plant phony hand grenades on the armored truck and steal the money when the guards ran away. He had heard of that approach used elsewhere.

"Yeah, okay, Steve," Kelly told him, rolling her eyes.

But when she left that day, Steve's interest in stealing from Loomis silently followed her. Kelly kept thinking about stealing from Loomis Fargo, about asking David if he would do it. Kelly had faith in Steve's ability to pull off the job. After all, he was always talking about his mysterious activities "up north," and he seemed to have a lot of money for someone without a full-time job.

In the following months, Steve mentioned the heist idea to Kelly a few more times. Still, until the middle of summer, it remained just a silly notion between the two of them. Then, on a late afternoon in August 1997, Kelly decided to page David at work and put the plan in motion.

Kelly felt she had compelling reasons to get out of her current life. Her marriage to Jimmy was failing; they had recently declared bankruptcy; she lived in an isolated mobile home; and despite a promotion at her security-guard job, she could not envision dramatically improving her lot. All she wanted was a house in the country, a swimming pool for her two kids, and a divorce.

Steve had told her to lie to David if that was what it took to make him steal the money, and that's what she did. She did not love David. She didn't want to move to Mexico. She didn't want her kids to grow up in a different country, on the run. But she wanted David to steal the money. So, in the back of her pickup truck two weeks before the heist, Kelly and David kissed passionately under the moon. He was thrilled.

One week before the heist, when Steve told her he had recruited Eric Payne and Scott Grant to help, Kelly did not object that the inner circle had nearly doubled. "You're the one with all the brains, Steve," she said. "You know what you're doing."

The group, minus David, met at the parking lot of Rose's Discount Store in Belmont, North Carolina, on the afternoon of the heist. When David said, over the phone, that he would be ready no earlier than seven o'clock that night, they crossed the street to the Textile Lanes bowling alley. While Kelly ate a cheeseburger and French fries, Eric Payne sidled up to her and asked, "Is this really gonna happen?"

"Yeah," Kelly said. "I don't believe it, but yeah, it's gonna happen."

Two weeks after the heist, Kelly was the only person in the United States who was speaking with David Ghantt.

By mid-October, the skinny redhead was not as skinny as he had been before he stole the money.

While the FBI checked up on Kelly back home, and while David's picture made the rounds in American newspapers, David lived the life of a rich international fugitive on the luscious white-sand beaches of Cancun, trying to keep a low profile among the tourist crowds that had flocked to the hotel zone since it opened in the mid-1970s.

He was not certain how much he had stolen from Loomis Fargo—he had not counted the money stacks when he grabbed them—but he estimated it was between $14 million and $15 million, and he eagerly awaited his one-third share. That was the deal. For the time being, he was skipping from hotel to hotel in Cancun and eating at least four meals a day. He learned to enjoy lobster, which he had never tried before.

Overall, though, his change in wealth was not quick to affect his tastes. His first two meals as a multimillion-dollar thief had been pizza at the airport in New Orleans and a Big Mac Combo at a Cancun McDonald's. His looks changed, though. He dyed his hair brown, bought some self-tanning spray, and had both ears pierced.

Free and rich in Cancun, David often thought back to his last morning in the mobile home 1,050 miles north in Kings Mountain, North Carolina. He remembered waking at five in the morning that day, taking a shower, putting on his gray Loomis Fargo uniform, making a pot of coffee, kissing his sleeping wife on the cheek, taking the garbage out, and leaving, closing the door on his family life.

He had been careful that week not to deviate from his normal routine. He even scheduled a dental appointment. But on the fateful morning, he packed three days' worth of clothes and his .45 caliber handgun and hopped into his 1996 Dodge Dakota pickup truck. He pulled into a service station and picked up a box of Marlboro Light 100s, a package of crackers, and a Cheerwine—the sweet, cherry-flavored carbonated drink of the South. Then he returned to the road, taking Interstate 85 into Charlotte. It was a forty-five-minute ride to work. He flipped the radio to his favorite morning station, which aired the *John Boy & Billy Big Show*, a Southern comedy talk show. The radio played "Take the Money and Run," by the Steve Miller Band.

During the day, as planned, Kelly drove to Loomis Fargo to pick up his gun, clothes, and cell phone, to give to David later.

Cancun's hotel zone is a fifteen-minute drive from the airport. After David's plane landed on October 5, the cabdriver took him down Kukulkan Boulevard, the main tourist strip. At first, the four-lane road passed just trees and power lines, but around a curve near kilometer marker 19, the beaches and turquoise sea came into view. This was why David had chosen Cancun as the place to wait out his heist share.

The cabdriver stopped at the Omni Hotel, a twelve-story flamingo-pink structure. At about $130 a night, it was not the most expensive hotel in town, but it was beautiful, its rooms looking out on to multiple sparkling pools, a large bar that served swimmers still in the water, the beach, and finally the Caribbean Sea.

David was mentally drained on October 5. After checking into the Omni, he slept for the better part of his first two days in Cancun. Then he began life as a happy tourist, complete with a shopping spree. David's clothes were meant for October in North Carolina, not in Mexico, and he was hot in long-sleeved shirts and pants. During his first three weeks, he bought a warm-weather wardrobe. He also bought three pairs of Ray-Ban sunglasses at $200 a pop; in a patriotic mood, he wanted one each in red, white, and blue. He also bought four pairs of python-skin cowboy boots. Mainly a T-shirt wearer, he started buying silk shirts.

He bought a third-row ticket to a bullfight and loved it, yelling "Toro! Toro!" with the crowd, though a beef-and-cheese snack from a vendor later gave him Montezuma's revenge, laying him up for three days, during which he ingested only Pepto-Bismol and Sprite.

Soon afterward, the amateur historian in him led him to tour the famous Mayan ruins at Chichen Itza, located about a hundred miles from Cancun, on Mexico's Yucatan Peninsula. The attractions included El Castillo, a pyramid built twelve hundred years earlier and shaped to represent the Mayan calendar, its eighteen terraces representing the eighteen twenty-day months of the Mayan year. Chichen Itza had a ball court called Juego de Pelota Principal. It was surrounded by temples where the losing captains were sacrificed in ancient days. The presence of the temples made the ball court an acoustical delight. Conversations could be heard more than two hundred feet away. Had David and Kelly lived in Mexico when they planned the theft, they would not have talked about it at Juego de Pelota Principal.

Ghantt loved it all. He reveled in the clubs and tourist-oriented malls of Kukulkan Boulevard. He found a favorite bar, Christine's, which had a huge dance floor and windows that looked on to the strip.

He did not expect to stay in Cancun for long. There were too many Americans, and he didn't want to be recognized. He planned to seek citizenship in another country, maybe Brazil. There, he would buy a fifty-five-foot boat. In his spare time, he would follow the heist investigation over the Internet. And he would send postcards with no return address to his relatives.

David spent his late-October days horseback riding, jet-skiing, and deep-sea fishing. He soared in an ultralight plane. It was like being a bird, he thought. He parasailed over the Caribbean, rising higher than the highest Cancun hotel, high enough that he could have yelled, "I stole $17 million!" and nobody would have heard. His view from above included the entire Cancun strip and the beautiful shades of blue sea. Knowing he had about $5 million coming his way made it seem impossible that anyone in the world could feel happier.

Most days, he woke up around ten-thirty, ate a big breakfast, sat on the beach, and decided what the hours ahead would include. He ate wherever he pleased, paying in cash at upscale restaurants. He had a favorite, Zandunga, a Caribbean-Mexican grill that served tasty spinach quesadillas, shrimp mounted on a coconut, and desserts of chocolate cake and flan. Mariachi bands performed while he looked at the evening sky over the Caribbean. He ate at Zandunga almost every other

David Ghantt spent time in several Mexican locations after the heist, including Cancun, Cozumel, and Playa del Carmen (*pictured above*).
CHARLOTTE OBSERVER

day. The waiters knew him by the name on his phony ID. They called him Mr. Mike and brought him bottles of Dos Equis beer. He made friends with a waiter named Aldo, who spoke some English and helped David find an apartment on the beach. When meeting Americans, he generally let them introduce themselves first and then lied about his coming from a different part of the country.

David felt no guilt or obligation toward Loomis Fargo and never questioned his decision to clean out the vault. He believed he would need about $4 million or $5 million to live comfortably the rest of his life, about one-third of what he stole. The rest of his share would be wired or smuggled to him soon, he figured. And Kelly would eventually come down to live with him, and they would spend the rest of their lives together and go through money like lunatics and get drunk and have sex and lie on the beach all day. It would be paradise. Kelly was the only person he had spoken with in North Carolina after the heist; he called her every Tuesday with a calling card at the pay phone by the Mount Holly convenience store. He told her he loved her and couldn't wait for her to come down. She told him she could not come just yet; the FBI thought she might be involved, and—who knew?—maybe they were tracking her.

As for Tammy, well, David figured she would move on. Their marriage was on the rocks anyway. He had worked too many hours, and they had not been seeing much of each other. When they did spend time together, they did not communicate well. But Kelly, he could talk to her about anything. And that kiss in the pickup truck had whetted his appetite for more. Though there was stress between them the day and evening of the crime, the future seemed rosy.

David's mind surged with excitement over the legend of David Ghantt, master thief. People would talk about David Ghantt for years, even decades, he figured. When they did, it would be with admiration, with envy, with intrigue.

Only one American had ever made off with a larger cash haul, and he, Philip Johnson, had made too many mistakes to be admired by the public. Johnson was violent, tying up his colleagues and threatening them. His robbery earlier in the year had lacked style. His capture was anything but glorious.

No, David would be thought of with the great ones—the D. B. Coopers, the Albert Spaggiaris, the Willie Suttons. They would be notable company.

David lacked the style of Cooper, who in 1971 had jumped out of a Boeing 727 jet, with $200,000 that wasn't his, somewhere between Portland, Oregon, and Seattle, Washington. Earlier, with the plane in the air, Cooper had threatened the worst unless authorities gave him the money and two parachutes when the commercial aircraft landed in Seattle. They did, and Cooper let the thirty-five passengers go free. Then he ordered the plane to fly again and jumped out somewhere over the Pacific Northwest. The crew members did not know exactly where he jumped, as they were forcibly locked in the cockpit. Less than $6,000 of the marked bills given to Cooper ever showed up—$5,880 was found buried without explanation in Washington State. Many suspected Cooper died soon after the theft. Still, to people who admired daring criminals, Cooper was heroic.

The same was true of Albert Spaggiari, who in July 1976 stole more than $8 million in money and valuables from the Société Générale bank in Nice, France. On the wall of the vault after the heist, he or a member of his gang wrote, "*Sans armes, sans haine, et sans violence*"—"Without weapons, without hatred, and without violence." The lack of bloodshed made it easier to admire criminals for their daring—or at least made it easier not to hate them. Spaggiari's notoriety stemmed from both his detailed planning—for several weeks, at night, his men dug a twenty-five-foot tunnel, measuring two feet by three feet, to access the vault—and his style. Before his fatigued crew members fled the bank, Spaggiari feted them with, of all things, a surprise meal. The joyous, shocked thieves were expecting anything but food at that point.

They dined, in the vault, on liver pâté, cheese, grapes, fruit, salami, and soup. Then, after taking their loot, they fled. Spaggiari was arrested months later when a low-level gang member tipped the police, but he escaped custody by jumping from a second-story magistrate's office during an interrogation. Authorities watched him being ridden away on a motorcycle. It was the last time they ever saw him alive.

David was no Spaggiari when it came to style. But when it came to the amount of cash successfully stolen without violence, David was Spaggiari times two-plus.

David also was far ahead of the legendary Willie Sutton, the best-known American bank robber, who, legend had it, when asked why he robbed banks, once replied, "That's where the money is." Though he threatened with weapons, Sutton went virtually his entire bank-robbing career without hurting anyone. From the 1940s to the 1960s, he robbed more than a hundred banks, usually disguised as either a police officer or a deliveryman. In total, he stole over $2 million. He was smooth with his victims, soothing them with his calm voice. But his cohorts occasionally betrayed him to police. He did three stints in prison totaling thirty-three years. In 1969, he became a free man. He worked as a security consultant.

By a multiple of almost nine, David had exceeded Willie Sutton's cash grabs in one act of criminal daring. Maybe, David hoped, others would talk about him with admiration. Maybe he would be known for his guts, for his brains, for his cagey mind.

The guts part seemed a certainty. Unlike the other thieves and robbers, David had pulled an inside job. He knew he would be a suspect right away, and the authorities had information on him from his employer. Inside jobs at banks and armored-car companies were not rare, but in the United States, only Philip Johnson had dared to steal more than David.

Bigger robberies had occurred abroad. In 1976, robbers stole an estimated $20 million to $50 million from safe-deposit boxes in Beirut at the British Bank of the Middle East. In Italy in 1984, five robbers with guns stole $21.8 million from Brink's Securmark in Rome.

Though excited by his new life, David was becoming more certain he could not return to the United States. He was not sure what his future identity would be—maybe Mike McKinney, or some character name from a novel by his favorite author, Tom Clancy—but it would not be David Ghantt. David Ghantt probably could never again get a driver's license, buy a house, install a phone, subscribe to a magazine, or use a credit card without David Ghantt's getting caught.

He figured Tammy would move on. He did not plan to call her or send her money.

But David's act of thievery had devastated Tammy, a sweet, pretty, brown-haired woman who had done nothing wrong to deserve this treatment. She was struggling both emotionally and financially. Her data-entry job could not pay the bills, so she tried to refinance their pickup truck for smaller monthly payments. But David's name was on the title along with hers, and the North Carolina Division of Motor Vehicles told her she could not remove his name without a court order. She hired a lawyer, who drew up the appropriate document: "That David Scott Ghantt has been accused and indicted in an alleged incident which took place on October 4, 1997 in Mecklenburg County, North Carolina in which a large amount of cash was taken from his . . . employer. That David Scott Ghantt has not been seen nor heard from since the time of the alleged incident and that he may be deceased."

A judge granted the order, and Tammy refinanced their loan. But the bills still were too high. The truck was soon repossessed.

Tammy also struggled to meet their mortgage payments on the mobile home. If worst came to worst, she could move in with her parents in Gastonia.

David's mother drove down from Hendersonville to stay with her during the week in the mobile home. On weekends, Tammy stayed at her parents' house, twenty minutes away. Going to sleep each night, she was tortured by thoughts of David. Was he dead? She wondered if the FBI had checked the Catawba River near where the Loomis van had been found. If he was alive, well, that alternative was not tremendously comforting either. Maybe he was being held hostage somewhere, by someone who had been standing in another room while David moved the money under the eyes of the security cameras. Otherwise, why wouldn't he have called her?

All she wanted was for him to be home. She wanted to fix him breakfast. She wanted to clean for him; their mobile home had never been so tidy as it was after he left, she was cleaning it so much.

She remembered how they first met, as teenage coworkers at the Winn-Dixie supermarket in Gastonia. She had been working the cash register one day and needed somebody to bag customers' groceries. A jokingly eager redhead had approached. "David Ghantt at your service, ma'am."

"You came to my rescue," she told him.

He liked that she thought of him as her rescuer. They began dating. He would wait outside the store for her shift to end and drive her home. After three months, she ended it. It was just one of those things, she told him. She dated other men, though she often thought back to him.

They rekindled their romance through letters while David was overseas in the army, and he proposed over the phone. He made it official after he was discharged, giving her a diamond ring, then getting on his knees and closing his eyes to ask if she would marry him.

They married on June 20, 1992, at Lakeview Church in the small town of McAdenville. Their wedding albums had such happy, funny pictures of that day. One of them had a photo of David with two letters taped to each shoe—*PL* on his right sole and *EH* on his left. His sisters had put them there as a joke gone wrong; they had meant to have his shoes spell out *HELP* when David knelt during the service, but they got the letters backwards. In another wedding picture, David was jokingly escaping through a church window. That one was not funny anymore.

After their wedding, the Ghantts lived in several places—in Hilton Head, South Carolina; Gastonia; and Kings Mountain. Tammy was content, especially when they bought the mobile home in Kings Mountain. She would come home and see David asleep on the couch, their cat, Rascals, snuggled on his chest. She and David would go on picnics, take weekend drives into the mountains ninety minutes away, and visit David's parents in Hendersonville. They considered having children in a few years, when Tammy turned thirty. Someday, they dreamed, she would open a tanning salon. He would open a hunting range.

Through her hardship, Tammy prayed. She prayed for David's safety, that he would come back so they could resume their lives. She prayed with David's mother, a religious woman who was helping Tammy get through this, and she prayed by herself, wherever she was.

Living the Life

TAMMY'S PRAYERS were not being answered, but only ten miles away, Steve and Michele Chambers seemed on the verge of getting everything they wanted.

In his mobile home the night of the heist, Steve had told his cohorts to lie low and not flagrantly spend the money. But he ignored his own advice. Even before the heist, he and Michele had itched to move up, though not out of the general area. In mid-October, they planned their move into the $635,000 house in Gaston County, into the gated community of Cramer Mountain.

With millions of dollars at their disposal, Steve and Michele obviously could have moved as far from the crime scene as they wanted. But rather than rent an apartment in Paris or buy a villa on the other side of the equator, they decided to stay close to home.

Their move to Gaston County, a twenty-minute drive from their mobile home in Lincoln County, might not seem an odd choice unless you're familiar with the Charlotte region. Gaston County, its culture shaped by generations of mill workers, was not nouveau riche. It was not even faux nouveau riche. Gaston was gritty.

True, Gaston had a growing middle class, but that did not hide its blue-collar feel. And in the Charlotte area, that blue-collar feel provided fodder for the comedy clubs, where a Gastonia putdown—"Hey, lemme guess, numb nuts, you're from Gastonia, right?"—guaranteed a laugh.

Gaston's textile industry was so huge in the early 1900s that the county's economy was slow to diversify in later decades, when textile plants faded and the rest of the Charlotte region modernized. Charlotte became a banking capital, while Gaston stayed a center of mill culture, with people bouncing from low-paying job to low-paying job. In 1995, more than one-third of the county's workers held jobs in manufacturing, twice the national average. Most of them lived quiet lives and did honorable work, making clothes, but to folks in Charlotte, the glimmering city of the New South, they were often looked down on as rednecks or lintheads—a pejorative based on the white lint that stuck to mill workers' clothes and hair and followed them out of the mill.

Most mill work did not pay well. In the 1990s, although fewer Gaston residents than in the past spent their careers working in mills, many people who went from one eight-dollar-an-hour job to another had worked in at least one.

Mill work was not always looked down on by North Carolina's middle class. In the 1920s, farmers from the mountainous western part of the state migrated in droves to Gaston County and other parts of the Charlotte area for mill salaries that were steady, if low. The mills, eager to keep their employees from jumping to competing mills, offered them housing around the factories, setting up their own little mill villages with company stores and even company chaplains.

Gaston's slowness to diversify its economy when its mills ceased prospering, combined with the rest of the region's rise, gave Gaston residents a certain wariness about Charlotte. Many Gaston residents thought it was just fine for those city folks to keep to themselves.

Charlotteans were hardly insulted by that mentality. Many stayed away from Gaston except to drive through it, west on Interstate 85 into the scenic mountains to visit attractions like Asheville and the touristy Biltmore Estate, the largest private residence in the United States. Besides, they could learn all they cared to about Gaston from the news, which always seemed to have reports of a shooting or stabbing or murder there.

Steve did not care about Gaston's reputation. He knew the area. He liked it. His and Michele's parents lived nearby. Most importantly, he wanted to show the people he had grown up with, the people who knew him as a small-timer, that he was a big shot. He could not do that by gallivanting in Paris or building a house in Beverly Hills.

On a mid-October afternoon, Michele showed up at her parents' house in Mount Holly. "I have a surprise," she told her mom, the pleasant Sandra Floyd. "I wanna show you something, where I'm gonna be moving."

Michele, her mother, and Michele's sister, Leigh Ann, got into a car, and Michele drove them to Cramer Mountain. They stopped at the security gate at the bottom.

Michele was moving into a place with a security gate? This had to be one of her crazy escapades, her mother figured. She could not possibly afford a house there. But Michele parked at 503 Stuart Ridge and led her mother and sister inside. Her mom was shocked. Alone with Michele in the bedroom, the disbelieving Sandra said to her daughter, "*I* can't afford something like this. You tell me how *you* can."

Michele excitedly said that by living in their mobile home for so long, she and Steve had been able to save gambling winnings. Sandra replied that it didn't seem like that would be enough.

Michele said they had gotten a financing deal from the interior designer who owned the place.

That was too much for Sandra to dissect. She decided to accept it. She did not ask the terms of the mortgage or the amount of the down payment. She assumed that Michele and Steve had put forth a down payment of $100,000 or so and had a reasonable, affordable mortgage. She did not do the math. She was not the type to ask questions about other people's finances.

Just because they would make their new life close to home didn't mean Steve and Michele were relinquishing travel. They did not fly, because Steve hated airplanes, but on October 24, three weeks after the heist, they took a train to New York with Eric Payne and his wife, Amy. The trip coincided with Michele's twenty-fifth birthday. Steve took $400,000 with him, getting his cousin Nathan to remove the money from a storage locker and deliver it to him. Steve did not know that Nathan also swiped $6,000 for himself.

Eric had been making good use of the money that Steve paid him the night of the theft. And since then, Steve had given him about $200,000 more. Eric had been at the monetary limit for his AT&T Family Federal Credit Union credit card at the time of the heist, but the following Friday, he deposited $9,000 into the account, paying off his $1,500 balance. The next day, he rented a new Cadillac on the credit card. He kept the car for nine days. Now, he was considering replacing his two-year-old pickup truck and also buying a motorcycle—a Harley-Davidson.

Up north on vacation, Eric and Steve did not discuss the details of the heist much. They went shopping with their wives in Manhattan, traveling in a white limousine that Steve rented for $1,000. At Bloomingdale's, Michele bought a brown Armani suit for $2,700. The limo, waiting outside, next took them to FAO Schwarz, the famous Fifth Avenue toy store. The group walked wide-eyed through the merchandise. Michele, gaga over the Barbie display, bought an antique Barbie and also picked up remote-control cars for her children.

Then they went to New Jersey, south on the Garden State Parkway to Atlantic City. Steve tipped the limo driver $1,000 when they arrived. Michele, a poker fiend, told the others she would not be one of those people who won a bundle and then lost it all; if she won ten grand, she said, she would stop gambling. Then she actually managed to win ten grand. She kept it.

Of course, ten grand to the Chamberses was, as Jackie Gleason would have said, a "mere bag of shells." Steve had $400,000 with him. The first night, he lost $12,000 playing blackjack, a game for which his great poker face was valueless. He was upset. But the next night, he won big, pounding Budweiser and getting so drunk that when he accidentally bumped into a man on the boardwalk, he handed him a few thousand dollars.

Overall, the rich got richer. Steve came away winning $60,000, paid out largely in $100 bills.

They had an eleven-hour train ride home.

Steve and Michele's house closing was scheduled for October 27, a Monday. They showed up at the office of their attorney, Jeff Guller, about two that afternoon, just after their return. Steve brought $53,000 worth of money orders and two black bags with $430,000 in cash—all in twenties—to buy the house. Sitting across the table from Guller, Steve unzipped one of the bags to show him it was full of money.

Guller did not act surprised to see the cash, despite having worked on Steve's worthless-check charges, which had seemed to indicate that large amounts of money came his way only through scheming. As an attorney, Guller was not supposed to knowingly help clients get away with crimes. But he had about two hundred clients at a given time, and he did not always remember the details of their cases. He didn't pry. He asked Steve where the money came from. Steve said he won a lot of it gambling in Atlantic City.

Days earlier, Guller had told Steve and Michele that if they were going to use that amount of cash to buy the house, they would have to fill out forms reporting the source of the money. For obvious reasons, Steve did not want to do that. Another possibility, Guller said, was securing checks for the transaction. They could still close on the $635,000 house as scheduled, but they would have to get those checks in the next week or so.

At the closing, Steve and Michele agreed to pay almost two-thirds up front. The sellers, Sally Stowe Abernathy and J. R. Abernathy, their attorney, and two real-estate agents were also present. Steve and Michele did not talk much during the fifteen-minute meeting. They signed the deed of trust.

The Abernathys, who owned an interior decorating business, were told that Steve and Michele could afford a $433,000 down payment for the house because Steve owned a string of laundromats and had played professional football. The sellers agreed to finance the remaining amount for $8,860 a month for two years. The Abernathys were profiting handsomely, having bought the home just two years earlier for $485,000. In an outside agreement, Steve and Michele would pay them about $40,000 in cash for pieces of furniture Michele liked that they had left in the house.

After the closing, Steve asked Guller if he could leave the two bags of cash in the lawyer's office for the time being. Guller said yes—a decision that would later haunt him—but added that if Steve did not come through with the checks, and soon, the cash would need to be used for the deal. Steve thought that he would be able to get the checks and that Guller's office was as good a place to put the cash bags as anywhere. And he figured that although Guller probably knew he had lived in a mobile home, he did not have to worry about being ratted out. He had not told Guller where the money came from, and he figured Guller would not ask the wrong questions. He figured Guller's office assistants would keep quiet as well.

Steve asked Guller about purchases and other ways to disburse money. Guller told him that keeping his deposits to under $10,000 in

This view shows the tiger-print stair runner in Steve and Michele's new home. The movers in the picture are packing up artwork shortly after the couple's arrest.
Robert Lahser / CHARLOTTE OBSERVER

cash could avoid banks' mandatory reports. Guller, who sensed that Chambers either was a hood or just wanted to be seen as one, figured it was no skin off his back to tell a client how government worked.

It was not the first time Steve had asked Guller this type of question. Steve once asked if a person could be indicted for simply lending money to criminals if he did not know what the debtors were using it for. Guller, not knowing exactly what Steve was talking about, responded that as long as Steve did not know, he was probably okay.

Steve had first noticed Guller four years earlier at a Gastonia restaurant called the Shrimp Boat, known around town almost as much for the sports-betting operation that its former owner had pleaded guilty to running from behind the counter as it was for its fantastic fried chicken. Steve never actually saw Guller bet there, but he figured Guller was shady and would keep his mouth shut.

Around town, Guller had served in leadership roles with the Gaston

County March of Dimes, the Red Cross, the Young Lawyers Association, and his synagogue. While playing football for East Mecklenburg High School, on the other side of the Catawba River, the five-foot-seven center and linebacker had won all-conference honors.

But the medical problems of a relative had contributed to debt problems. Guller's practice had been in trouble with the law and under the scrutiny of the State Bar Association. In 1989, his second wife pleaded guilty to embezzling from escrow accounts that clients had established with Guller's practice. The State Bar Association ruled that Guller was indirectly responsible, allowing that he did not know about the theft. He kept practicing, building a reputation for combativeness in favor of his clients.

Steve now had a $433,000 challenge. He had to secure that amount in checks or money orders for the down payment. His game plan was to pay other people to get the checks for him, "lending" them briefcases of cash, from which the helpers would buy Steve money orders or cashier's checks that he would use for the house purchase. For their troubles, the helpers would get from 5 to 10 percent of the check amounts, in cash.

As part of these house-purchasing efforts came one of Steve and Michele's most startling cash indiscretions, days after the closing. Michele dwarfed her previous breach of bank etiquette when she walked into the Wachovia Bank in Belmont with $200,000 in cash inside a briefcase. She had $150,000 in hundreds, $25,000 in fifties, and $25,000 in twenties. She asked the teller for an official bank check, payable to herself under her former married name, Shelley Harris. The bank declined.

Then Steve and Michele drove an hour north to Salisbury, North Carolina, to a First Union National Bank. There, they had an accommodating teller named Kim Goodman. She knew the Chamberses. In fact, she had been expecting their visit. She and her husband, Mike

Goodman—a friend of Steve's—had previously agreed that she would accept their check transaction in return for Steve's paying $10,000 in cash to Kim on her lunch break that day. She convinced her superiors the deal was legitimate, and then filed the necessary paperwork for all cash transactions over $10,000.

By the end of the first week of November, Steve also obtained an $80,000 cashier's check with help from John Hodge and a $100,000 check with help from John's son Calvin, a friend of Steve's. Steve claimed he needed their help because he didn't have a checking or savings account.

These efforts were more discrete. Days after the closing, Steve put $108,000 in a briefcase and hauled it to a Burger King in the small town of Dallas, North Carolina, where Calvin Hodge waited for him. Hodge, who drove an ice-cream truck, had agreed to convert cash into a check at his bank in Dallas. He would keep the extra $8,000 as a fee.

The checks and money orders went into Guller's escrow account at First Citizens Bank. On November 6, the money was used as the down payment. As a legal fee for handling the house closing, Steve paid Guller $1,000.

The pair had more business together. On November 13 at the Gaston County Courthouse, Guller represented Steve when he pled guilty to forty-two counts of obtaining property by false pretenses. Steve avoided state prison, getting off with five years' probation, community service, restitution, and an $800 fine. Also, he would carry the convictions on his record.

While discussing the case before the plea, Steve bragged to Guller that he was "pretty slick" to have performed the check-writing scheme at all.

"Not slick enough," Guller shot back. "You're not smart. You're a distinctive-looking guy. You're six feet tall, 250 or 260 pounds, with a beard. How are people not going to recognize you?"

Steve told Guller he was considering paying his $30,000 of restitution for the worthless checks all at once. Did that make sense? Or should he keep to the drawn-out payment schedule suggested by the court?

Guller told him to keep to the schedule.

Those who opened the front door to Steve and Michele's new home saw a curved staircase with a faux tiger-skin stair runner. In the foyer, backdropped by a tan marble floor and mauve-and-black wallpaper, stood a Haddorff grand piano, a bronze statue of a beautiful woman, and a large beveled mirror with a leopard-fabric frame. There also were gold-framed paintings of fruit and flowers.

To the left was the dining room, which had fancy china on a polished wooden table and a bust of Caesar on a pedestal. From there, a right turn led into the huge kitchen, which had abundant counter space. The kitchen also featured a statue of a fat chef, a brass pineapple, a ceramic white elephant, and oil paintings of a leopard and an elephant.

No wall separated the kitchen from the living room, where the decorations included gold-framed oil paintings of zebras, prints of elephants, and an oil painting of a street in Italy. There also was a gas-log fireplace, a wooden entertainment center, a goose decoy, and a statue of a horse. On the shelves were intriguing bookends—statuettes of nude women.

Perhaps the most stunning part of the house was the master bedroom, which was sunken six steps from the rest of the first floor. The simple, off-white decor and leather-padded headboard had an air of ritz, as did the clear-glass bedroom fireplace that looked on to a sunken whirlpool surrounded by four fluted columns in the cream-colored bathroom. The whirlpool was six feet in diameter and had brass faucets. And if filling the tub took too long, there was always the marble-walled walk-in shower, which measured six feet by six feet.

Next to the master bedroom was the study, which had a Baccarat crystal chandelier hanging from the ceiling and a black-and-gold family crest on the wall. There was also a beautiful eight-drawer desk for

Steve to conduct his business, and a leather chair behind it. His office decor included a handmade Civil War chess set and bookends shaped like dogs and lions.

The well-furnished basement had a game room and a wine cellar. To the right of the stairs was a glossy, black-tiled bar, on which sat a clown-faced lava lamp. Steve and Michele occasionally placed a velvet Elvis Presley portrait by the bar. They hadn't bought the velvet Elvis themselves. It was a gag gift for Sally Stowe Abernathy, the previous owner, from one of her relatives. She had left it in the house when she moved. Steve and Michele kept Corona and Coors Lite beer behind the bar. The game-room walls were decorated with plaques commemorating Steve's supposed former team, the Dallas Cowboys, and a framed print of Robert E. Lee. The jewel of the room was a pool table that cost just under $10,000. There also was a tanning bed. A door from the game room opened into the wine cellar, which had a brick floor, gold wallpaper, and about three hundred square feet of space.

Outside, Michele and Steve added a $10,000 fence. It gave them privacy and allowed their dogs—a basset hound named Dallas and a poodle named Ty Cobb—to play outside. The couple enjoyed the dogs and sometimes playfully addressed the poodle as "you little bastard," as befit the man for whom it was named, the famous Detroit Tigers outfielder of the early twentieth century. Michele decided to discontinue the practice one day after hearing a toddler relative exclaim, "Ty Cobb, you wittle bastard!"

Among the guests at Steve and Michele's first Halloween party as millionaires was Kelly Campbell, who purchased a Cleopatra costume but was told at the last minute not to wear it because others would not have costumes. Kelly was a frequent visitor to the house, playing pool and poker with Steve with fresh stacks of dollar bills.

But though she had helped organize the heist by serving as the link between Steve and David—and, of course, by recruiting David—Kelly was playing a subordinate role to Steve in the aftermath. Steve was making all the decisions about where to hide the money and about who got what. Kelly still believed the money was "up north" somewhere with Steve's crooked bankers. She was supposed to get one-third of the loot, but she figured she would not ask Steve for it until the FBI had left her alone for a while.

Her main involvement after the heist, besides spending more money than she ever had before, was talking with Ghantt on the phone and then, later, telling Steve what he said. Kelly did not plan to move to Mexico with him, though she still let him think she did—maybe in December, when things quieted down, she said. Telling him this kept the situation stable. In reality, she wanted to buy a new place of her own not far from her family. She looked at a two-story home for sale in Bessemer City, in Gaston County, and also considered moving outside the county.

David, of course, had no clue that his murder was being considered. So far, Kelly had managed to talk Steve out of it. But they had discussed various possibilities, including having David injected with Clorox. The bleach would kill him, they figured. Kelly was not certain she wanted David killed—he was her friend—and Steve was not sure it would actually happen, but they were talking about it.

For a Halloween party at a fancy new house, this was a low-key gathering. Kelly, Steve, Michele, Eric and Amy Payne, and a few others drank beer, talked, and listened to music. Steve took Kelly aside and brought up the murder plan again. If they did not go forward with the murder, Ghantt was bound to lead the FBI back to the rest of them, he said.

Kelly was high and gave in. "Just do whatever you need to do," she said, salving her conscience with more marijuana.

An occasional guest at the house was Amy Grigg, the fiancée of

Steve's cousin Nathan Grant. She was supposed to keep an eye on the money at Lincoln Self Storage. In early November, the company sent her a letter saying that if she did not pay the monthly fee, it would open the locker and sell the contents. Amy asked her mother, Kathy, to go pay the bill. Kathy did so and brought home the receipt.

Early November brought an important house guest when Mike McKinney, the original bearer of the ID David was now using, flew in from Illinois. Over the phone, Steve had told McKinney only that he had a job for him, that he needed help involving a man hiding in Mexico because of a failed drug-related shooting.

McKinney was impressed by Steve's new digs. But things seemed quiet at the Chambers castle. McKinney had expected a party for Steve's thirtieth birthday, but it was just McKinney and Steve's family.

Details of the murder-for-hire broke the calm. Steve told McKinney that his previous $250,000 offer, first made in Indiana the previous month, involved killing the man hiding in Mexico. Steve would pay one-half up front. Steve did not say where he got all this money from, and McKinney didn't ask.

McKinney had never been a hit man before. He did not have a criminal record for *any* violence. In fact, he had been a smart, popular student at his high school in Bridgeport, Illinois, graduating with a GPA over 3.2. McKinney, who stood six-foot-four, weighed a slim two hundred pounds, and had a close-cut brown beard, joined the marines after some community college. He was a TOW gunner with a heavy-weapons platoon—First Battalion, Second Marine Company.

McKinney repeated his willingness to go along with Steve's $250,000 offer. The money impressed him enough that he ignored the danger.

The plan would involve visiting Mexico, McKinney was told. The target, known to McKinney only as Scott, would meet him thinking he would be getting money, so McKinney would take cash in case there was no good opportunity to commit the murder. In that case, he would give Scott the money as cover and maybe discuss ways to move Scott to a country without an extradition treaty.

A few evenings later, after a meal, Michele and Steve were driving down Charlotte's Independence Boulevard past one giant commercial establishment after another—places selling electronics merchandise, chain restaurants, home-supply stores, appliance retailers, and car dealerships. Michele spotted a sporty white BMW passing them. "Look at that," she said to Steve. "Isn't that cute?"

"Yeah, it's okay," Steve said.

The car was a BMW Z-3 roadster, a convertible.

A few days later, while on another drive down Independence Boulevard, Steve turned into the BMW dealership. He said to his wife, "Do you want to drive one?"

She took it for a test drive down Independence. It felt good. Very good. They paid for it in cash—$27,000 in cash.

Looking for another way to hide or launder his money, Steve bought a furniture business located in downtown Gastonia, across the street from the county courthouse. The seller was an acquaintance of Steve's named Michael Staley, who had run the store as a discount outlet. Staley wanted $75,000 for the store, and when Steve declined that price, they agreed that Steve would pay $25,000 up front and an undetermined amount later. They wrote nothing down about future payments. Staley was recovering from stomach surgery and wanted as little trouble from the transaction as possible. He wanted to close the deal.

Steve changed the store's name from Furniture Discount Center to M&S Furniture, for Michele and Steve. He closed the store temporarily to put in a new concrete floor, lay carpet, and redo the bathroom. He also replaced the discount inventory with higher-end merchandise. Michele drove to area newspapers to buy ads for the new store and even purchased radio spots on a local station.

Steve wanted Staley and his mother, Ruth, who had worked part-time at the store, to stay around as employees. Mike Staley decided he didn't want to work there. His mother accepted the offer, though.

One day, Ruth Staley asked Steve how he could afford the more expensive furniture. Steve said he was an ex-football player and that he was great at gambling, that he could win thousands of dollars at blackjack at casinos in Las Vegas and Atlantic City.

For the most part, Kelly Campbell was enjoying her new riches. No, she had not seen anywhere close to one-third of the stolen money, but she had seen six figures. For the first time in her life, she could buy things without worrying about a budget. Her once-miniscule bank account at the AT&T Family Federal Credit Union was growing, too. She had deposited $800 two days after the heist and $1,715 a week later. And she was thinking about buying a minivan.

The FBI interviews right after the heist still had her nervous in early November. When she decided it was time to buy the minivan, she asked Steve to come with her and register it under a different name, so it would not draw attention.

It was November 13 when Steve and Kelly drove to the Harrelson Toyota dealership in Fort Mill, South Carolina, just south of Charlotte. They had $16,000 with them, all in twenty-dollar bills. Steve introduced himself as Robert Dean Wilson. It was an alias he had used before. They sat down with the salesman to fill out paperwork for a Toyota Sienna XLE minivan. The papers required a social security number for Robert Dean Wilson, so Steve made one up off the top of his head. On the loan application, Steve put down his place of employment as Chambers Industries.

A few days later, Kelly and Steve returned to Harrelson Toyota to pay off the rest of the minivan—with $14,220 in twenty-dollar bills.

A week later, for Thanksgiving, both sets of spouses—Kelly and Jimmy and Steve and Michele—drove together to Atlantic City for a few days of fun. It was Steve's second trip there in a month. He drove. When they arrived, they gambled with large amounts of money, strolled the famous boardwalk, and went shopping. They stayed at the Hilton Hotel. Kelly bought leather coats for herself and Jimmy and shopped at a Warner Brothers store for her children. As they gambled, Steve gave a $100 chip to a drink server as a tip.

In their hotel room, Jimmy noticed Kelly unzip a duffel bag full of cash. She told him Steve and Michele had a bag just like it.

Jimmy asked his wife if the money was from the Loomis Fargo theft.

She said yes.

He had figured as much, he said. Angry, he left the hotel room. Unfortunately, he was in no position to seriously protest, because Steve and Michele were his ride back to North Carolina.

Tercel to BMW

LOOMIS FARGO WANTED to make somebody else rich. Soon after the heist, the company posted a $500,000 reward for information leading to an arrest or conviction in the case, and people called with tips. In mid-November, the company still held out hope a tip would produce results.

Loomis, Fargo & Co. was formed in 1996 when a Chicago-based Borg-Warner Security Corporation, which owned Wells Fargo Armored Services, merged with Dallas-based Wingate Partners, which owned Loomis Armored. The new company, which employed eighty-five hundred people, was owned 51 percent by Loomis shareholders and 49 percent by Borg-Warner Security.

The roots of the armored-transport industry stretch to the mid-1800s, during the California gold rush, when horse-drawn carriages were counted on to safely transport gold. With the rise of railroads later in the century, trains became the favored way to move cash.

Modern practices date to the 1920s, when Brink's Express—now called Brink's Inc., the largest armored-transport company in the United States but back then a freight company—leased a school bus fortified with steel to Chicago companies transporting large amounts of cash. The idea caught on. Armored vehicles were faster and safer than the armed couriers then working in cities, and they were less vulnerable to robberies than trains.

The need for armored cars increased dramatically after World War II, when suburbanization led to the placement of bank branches outside of cities, which increased the need for cash transport. Decades later, the large armored-car companies were transporting more than $500 million each day.

Armored-car companies operate with slim profit margins because banks—which make up much of their business—do not pay the companies more than they have to. This is partially because as long as the movement of their money is insured—which it is, by the armored-car companies—bank officials care little about who moves it.

Loomis Fargo's announcement about its reward, combined with the coverage on *America's Most Wanted*—the network replayed the Ghantt segment to make up for the ball-game snafu—led to a barrage of tips. But none panned out. Many of the leads seemed inspired by non-heist-related pettiness.

"He just bought a BMW, and his last car was a Tercel!"

"The family down the street, they're doing quite a bit of traveling lately, much more than usual."

The agents had to check these out. But it was so much easier to call the FBI to say you suspected the guy down the street than it was to prove the guy down the street was in on the heist.

In the last days of October, a legal assistant from Jeff Guller's office called and told the hotline operator that a man named Steve Chambers had an extremely large amount of cash stashed in her employer's office, and that it seemed suspicious, given the heist. The *America's Most Wanted* operator replied that they were not looking for anybody named

Steve Chambers. That was the end of it.

The FBI received permission from a federal judge to monitor the telephone lines of Kelly Campbell, Tammy Ghantt, and Nancy Ghantt, David's sister. The phone-monitoring devices, called "pen registers," show how long telephone calls last, and who calls whom. Pen registers do not involve recording phone calls; that is the province of wiretaps, considered much larger infringements on citizens' privacy and harder for the FBI to win permission to use. To have a judge allow a wiretap in this case, the FBI needed much more evidence. It would also have to prove that agents already had exhausted less intrusive approaches.

The judge's order gave the FBI permission for two months of pen registers. Meanwhile, the United States Attorney's Office subpoenaed toll records, which show records of old calls—who made them and how long they lasted.

It seemed that Kelly Campbell had lied to the FBI. Toll records showed that the numbers registered to Campbell and Ghantt had telephone contact on October 3 and October 4, the day of the heist.

Michele Chambers loved her BMW Z-3, which reflected a post-heist lifestyle that would draw her unwanted attention.
Charlotte Observer

Campbell told the agents she hadn't talked to Ghantt for at least two or three weeks before the theft. Of course, she still was not exhibiting a rich lifestyle, so if she had heist money, apparently she was not spending it.

Agents also began to suspect that Kelly had lied when she told them she and David smoked marijuana together. Loomis officials had since told the FBI that Ghantt passed his company drug tests.

Supervisors in Charlotte's FBI office scaled back the investigation at the end of October. Womble, Rozzi, and the rest of Squad Six stayed focused on the heist, but Wydra, Mueller, and their Squad Four colleagues went back to working white-collar cases.

Halloween came and went without any breaks in the case. Then, in the second week of November, publicity over the heist began bearing fruit. An anonymous caller told the FBI she knew a woman named Michele Chambers who had just moved into an expensive house she should not have been able to afford.

A few days later, on November 12, the FBI received another intriguing call, about Chambers and her husband, Steve. The anonymous caller said that the couple had been living in a mobile home in Lincoln County until two weeks earlier, and that Steve and Michele had just bought a large, expensive house at the exclusive Cramer Mountain Country Club in Gaston County. The caller had no proof that they were involved in the heist, but the whole thing seemed suspicious because neither Steve nor Michele had a steady job. Steve was just a small-time crook who had been involved in holding stolen property, the caller said. When the caller had asked Michele how they could buy such a big house, Michele beat around the bush, saying that the seller and an attorney were taking care of things.

None of which proved, of course, that Steve Chambers was involved in the heist. His newfound cash could have been drug money, or gambling winnings, or who knew what. But the feds planned to keep an eye on him. The supervisors assigned John Wydra to check out the Chamberses and their house purchase, figuring Wydra's experience investigating money laundering and financial transactions would be helpful.

Wydra drove from Charlotte to Gastonia, where the Gaston County Courthouse sat downtown across the street from a barbershop and a furniture store, to check the deed for the house transaction. As he walked up the steps of the courthouse, Wydra was unaware that Steve and Michele Chambers were starting up their furniture business a few hundred feet away.

Inside the courthouse, records showed that Steve and Michele's new house cost $635,000 and that they had paid most of it down, needing a loan for less than $200,000 of the purchase price. Wydra also researched their criminal records and learned of Steve's guilty plea to forty-two counts of obtaining property by false pretenses. The records included a series of aliases Chambers used for the scams, and Wydra punched these into the FBI's database. They were names that would not ordinarily turn heads—Robert Dean Wilson, Steven Jeffcoat. The records showed Chambers was a scam artist but did not suggest he was the type to attempt a $17 million heist.

On November 18, the FBI received another confidential call that stood out. It was about Eric Payne. According to the caller, Payne had gone on vacation for two weeks starting the day after the heist, and was now spending more money than he could afford on his salary. He had just bought a new Chevy Tahoe and had explained his new wealth as an inheritance. Plus, the informant said, he worked at Reynolds & Reynolds, located less than a mile from the wooded area where the Loomis van had been found two days after the theft.

Dick Womble dealt with this call. He checked records to see if any of Payne's relatives had recently died. They had not. That made his inheritance excuse seem sketchy. Womble also drove to Reynolds & Reynolds and discretely spoke with people there. He learned that Payne had attended East Gaston High School. He also learned that Steve

Chambers had briefly worked at Reynolds & Reynolds, under different ownership, years earlier.

The FBI now knew that Steve Chambers and Eric Payne, independently, were spending a lot of money. But the agents had no solid way to tie them together—besides knowing both had worked at Reynolds & Reynolds and attended East Gaston High School—or to tie them to David Ghantt or Kelly Campbell. The agents didn't even know if Chambers and Payne were spending Loomis money. The proximity of Payne's workplace to the van seemed a possible indication of something, but maybe it was just a coincidence. The feds lacked a definite connection.

A link, if only a minor one, came soon after the informants' calls, when agents obtained permission for pen registers and permission to subpoena toll records of the phone belonging to Steve Chambers. They noticed continued phone contact between Payne and Chambers. They also noticed that Jeff Guller, who had called them the week after the heist about Kelly Campbell's polygraph, had phone contact with Chambers the very next day. Maybe Chambers and Campbell knew each other. Maybe Guller was involved. Of course, he was an attorney, so maybe he just happened to represent both of them. The connection was certainly nothing to seek an arrest warrant on. For the first time, however, the FBI could find a way to link Steve Chambers to Kelly Campbell.

The FBI cross-checked every new name with the monthly reports of the Financial Crimes Enforcement Network. Known as FINCEN, the agency coordinates information in Suspicious Activity Reports filed by banks nationwide. The FBI hoped Kelly Campbell or Steve Chambers or Eric Payne would show up on FINCEN's list, but since the reports often take two or three months to climb official channels back to the FBI, that had not happened yet. A report taken in October would not reach agents until mid-December or later.

Thanksgiving came, Thanksgiving went, and despite all the informants and interviews, the FBI still had no clue if David Ghantt was dead or alive. And if he was alive, the agents had no idea where he might be. Idaho? Mexico? Venezuela? New York? He could have been anywhere, even in Charlotte.

Anxious for a new approach, the FBI engaged the inexact science of behavior profiling. Dick Womble and Mark Rozzi drove from Charlotte to Stafford, Virginia, to the FBI's National Center for Analysis of Violent Crimes. There, they talked to profiling experts.

The behavioral analysis unit focused on finding serial killers, rapists, and kidnapers, stockpiling databases and tips from crimes across the country to devise theories on the next steps of missing criminals with similar backgrounds. David Ghantt did not fit the bill of what the unit normally studied, but the feds figured the experts' eyes wouldn't hurt. Womble and Rozzi had already discussed the case with the unit's experts over the phone, but they wanted to talk with them in person.

From Womble and Rozzi, the experts at the center learned about Ghantt's background, his family, his physical build. The agents mentioned that Ghantt's relatives and friends said he liked reading about counterintelligence and the FBI. They mentioned that Ghantt's coworkers said he complained about his marriage, and that those coworkers suspected an affair between Ghantt and Kelly Campbell. They mentioned that the coworkers said Ghantt frequently criticized Philip Johnson—the man who had pulled the bigger heist in Jacksonville—and that Ghantt would say things like, "Where that guy screwed up was, he stuck around. He should've cut all ties."

The unit's experts thought it over. Ghantt's physical build suggested he probably could not have moved all the money by himself, so he probably had help with the crime, the experts told Rozzi and Womble. Many of Ghantt's favorite novels had plots with spies fleeing to Central and South America, so perhaps he was somewhere there, trying to live the fascinating life of one of the characters and striving to not repeat the mistake of Philip Johnson by coming back. Ghantt's marriage history gave reason to suspect there was a woman involved, the experts said. Given what the agents had learned about his wife, it probably was not she. Maybe it was Kelly Campbell.

The conclusions seemed simple to have come from behavior-profiling experts, but Rozzi and Womble were glad, at least, that the Charlotte bureau seemed on the right track. Whether that would lead to an arrest, nobody knew, but at least they felt they were doing what good investigators should be doing and had drawn reasonable preliminary conclusions.

The agents were performing periodic physical surveillance on Kelly Campbell. In mid-December, they learned she was driving a new Toyota minivan. They discretely jotted down the license plate number. Over the next several days, they tracked down the purchase and registration information.

Womble and Rozzi, back in Charlotte from Virginia, tried their luck on Campbell, calling her on December 29 to set up a meeting to ask about Ghantt and to see if she would take a lie-detector test. Campbell was busy. Her son was recovering from appendicitis, so she could not meet the morning the agents called. Instead, they arranged to meet later in the day, at the Gaston Mall.

Once there, they sat down over coffee, making small talk about Kelly's son's condition. Then they got down to business.

"We're still trying to locate David Ghantt," Womble told her.

Kelly stayed true to her prior story, saying she had no idea where he was.

"We think there's more to this than you're telling us," Womble said, not sharing the FBI's current knowledge, through toll records, about her previous lies concerning whether or not she had talked to Ghantt before the heist. "Would you take a polygraph for us?"

During the fifteen minutes they were together at the mall, Kelly's cell phone and pager were ringing and buzzing almost constantly, but she did not respond to them. Womble and Rozzi managed to hide their wonder at this, but they showed some disappointment when she told them to call her attorney, Jeff Guller, with their questions. They shook hands with her, and she left. Neither agent believed she would ever take a polygraph for them.

On December 28, a man called the FBI about Steve Chambers. He said he had never met Chambers, but he knew Mike Staley, who had sold Chambers his furniture store in Gastonia. The caller had talked with Staley, who said he had been inside Steve's new house and had seen a bag so heavy with twenty-dollar bills that Steve had trouble lifting it. The caller suspected Chambers was in on the heist.

For the FBI, it was another tip that something was awry with Chambers.

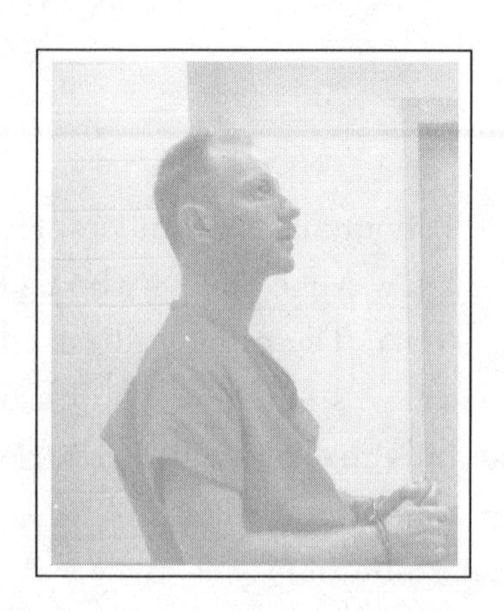

Dead Man in Mexico?

THE INTERNATIONAL FUGITIVE could last only so long on $25,000. October days of lobster and parasailing and fancy hotels quickly ate away at David Ghantt's first heist installment. In the first week of November, he realized he needed more cash. It was to his extreme displeasure that he had yet to receive his one-third share of the loot.

The man who pulled off the second-largest heist in United States history was reduced to eating homemade grilled cheese sandwiches and pasta, just in case his expected money did not arrive soon. He was renting an apartment with a kitchen for about $800 a month. It was near Cancun's beach, just off Kukulkan Boulevard.

He was not alone. He had met a woman named Lindsey, who was twenty-four, blond, and Canadian, as far as David knew. He had met her at Christine's. As far as Lindsey knew, David was a small-time drug dealer from the States, and his name was not David, it was Mike McKinney. His shadiness did not bother her—every so often, she somehow popped up with a wad of cash herself.

The Cancun couple drank at local clubs and went scuba diving; he had bought them $3,000 worth of diving equipment and a $900 navigational computer. She moved in with him in mid-November after getting kicked out of her own place. They coexisted with different decorating styles—he put up a Pittsburgh Steelers pennant, while she brought home a picture of a bullfighter. They threw parties. Her friends, who were Ecstasy dealers, would show up. David did not indulge in their wares, but he enjoyed their company.

One of Lindsey's friends worked for a car-rental company. One day, David and Lindsey rented a Volkswagen Beetle and went driving outside Cancun, joyriding at seventy-five miles per hour on roads with lower posted speeds. It was hardly his most serious transgression of the year. Still, a local police officer's siren blared behind them.

As they were stopped on the side of the road, David was confident his Michael McKinney ID would stand up to scrutiny. Nobody had given him trouble over it. He rolled down his window as the officer walked up to the car.

"It's very hot today, sir," the officer said. "I'd like a drink."

David had heard about the police in Mexico. Without a word, he placed $60 in the ticket book the officer was holding out to him.

"Have a nice day," the officer said before he drove away and left them to enjoy themselves.

The Cancun fling was only so fulfilling. From a pay phone, David called Kelly Campbell on Tuesdays using a calling card. He reached her at various pay phones to demand a first installment of the rest of his money. He wanted $50,000 as soon as possible, he told her in early November.

Kelly relayed his words to Steve, who told her to tell David they would send a man known as Bruno to Cancun with cash for him. She relayed the information to David, who suggested they meet at a place called the Rainforest Café.

In North Carolina, the hit man's trip to Mexico to meet David almost ended before it began. The real Mike McKinney, a.k.a. Bruno, was not a very discrete smuggler. In the men's bathroom at Charlotte/ Douglas International Airport, he bundled $10,000 of heist money, given to him by Steve, inside the waist of his jeans to prepare for his walk through the metal detector. Then, as he walked out of the bathroom, he felt the money falling down his pants! He scurried back inside the bathroom, his eyes widening as he envisioned police officers swarming around him. Luck was on his side. The money stayed above his ankles. He readjusted the cash into more manageable stacks and continued his adventure.

When the plane landed in Cancun, McKinney booked a room at the Mex Hotel and went to the Rainforest Café, where he had been told to meet "Scott," who he knew was using his identification papers. McKinney thought the guy was hiding in Mexico because he shot somebody; that's what Steve had told him.

But McKinney could not find him. He scanned the Rainforest Café, a restaurant and tourist store with a faux rain-forest motif that included jungle noises. He was looking for a man who, he had been told, was six feet tall with red or blond hair and weighed between 130 and 160 pounds. McKinney knew little else about the guy, having never even seen a picture. Ghantt was there, but McKinney didn't see him. He left, came back later, and still could not find his man.

Around town, he asked people who spoke English if they knew anyone named Mike.

What does an aspiring hit man do when he can't find his target? McKinney went on a spending spree. First, he bought T-shirts and shorts, having arrived only with long-sleeved shirts and pants. Then he went out drinking and meeting women, and drinking and jet-skiing, and drinking and sunbathing, and meeting more women. He visited Cancun bars like Dady Rock, where the dancing often turned wild, and La Boom, which had frequent bikini contests.

He called Steve and said he was having no luck. Steve told him to fly back to North Carolina, where they would regroup.

McKinney would catch a plane north the next day. This night, he would go out drinking.

While McKinney was getting piss drunk, David was getting pissed off. The man with the tan from a can wanted his money. On the phone, he told Kelly to have Bruno bring it to a room at the Villa Marlin beachfront complex of apartments and condominiums in Cancun, which David had rented just for this contact. He did not want anybody up north to know where he was really living, in case they got arrested.

A few days after McKinney returned to North Carolina, he flew back to Cancun, again with instructions to kill, if possible. This time, he made it through the airport's metal detector without any near-mishaps, having more skillfully bundled the money in stacks of twenty-dollar bills, each stack containing two grand. Steve Chambers, in a meeting with McKinney at a hotel in downtown Charlotte, had told McKinney to go to the Villa Marlin's room 202.

At about six o'clock on a mid-November morning, McKinney found the tan-and-pink stucco Villa Marlin complex and knocked on the door of room 202. A woman answered. She did not speak English. His man was not inside. McKinney had the wrong room.

He called Steve, who had made a mistake; he meant to say room 206. He told McKinney to try again. Steve also temporarily called off the murder plan.

That night, the hit man spent more than $1,000 of the money meant for his target.

The next morning, at five-thirty, McKinney knocked on the right door. David opened it. McKinney asked, "You lookin' for help from Charlotte?"

David let him in. McKinney dropped $8,500 in twenties on David's bed. David could not believe that was all he was getting. "That's it? That's it? What the fuck is this? There's nothing else?"

"That's all they gave me," McKinney said.

David said he wanted $50,000.

"This is what they gave me. This is what you get," McKinney said. He explained how he had been given the wrong room number earlier.

"Yeah, that's par for the course," David said with disgust as McKinney turned around and left.

David was stunned. At this pace, it would take more than five hundred separate cash deliveries for him to get his $5 million. But he didn't waste time doing the math. Within a few minutes of Bruno's departure, he realized for the first time that he might never see his share of the stolen millions. He lay on his bed staring at the ceiling, straining to give his cohorts up north the benefit of the doubt. Maybe there were difficulties he did not know about, he hoped. Maybe they would bring much more next time.

Frustrated millionaire or not, David no longer had to scrounge for food. His early-November days of pasta and grilled cheese were over. He was still worried about getting his money, but at least he had enough to eat out.

A week after the first cash delivery, Bruno came to Cancun again, this time meeting David in a hotel restaurant. Under a table, Bruno gave him a brown paper bag and left. David finished his meal and returned to his room. He opened the bag and saw only $8,500 inside. "What the hell is this?" he yelled.

He paged Kelly to let her know he would be calling. He shouted at her on the phone: "What the hell is this shit?"

Kelly asked, "Did you get your money?"

"Yeah, I did," David said. "I got eight grand. I wanted eighty."

Kelly said she would speak to Steve.

David again tried to rationalize. Chances were he would get his share of the loot if he waited a little bit longer, he told himself. It could have been worse. Meanwhile, he tried once more to get Kelly to

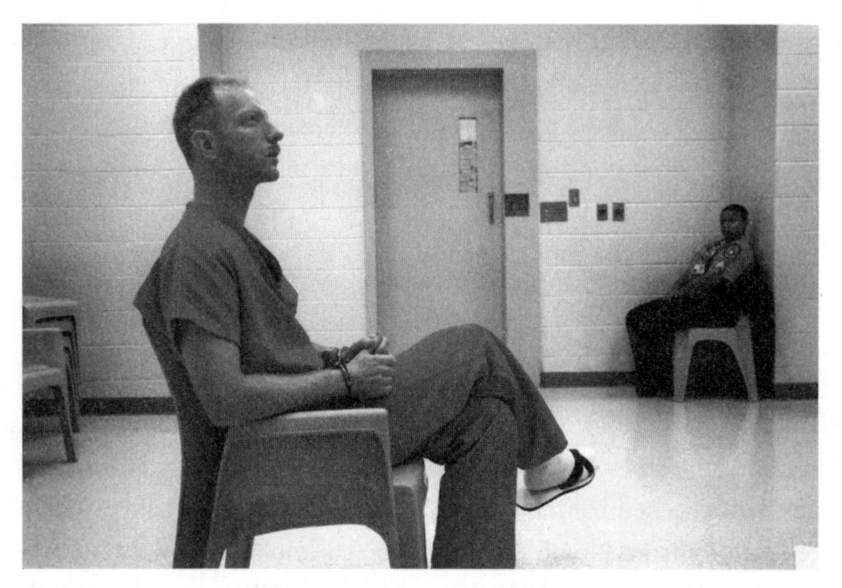

In November, David Ghantt began to worry that he would not get his expected heist share.
Laura Mueller / CHARLOTTE OBSERVER

move down with him. He told her over the phone that he loved her and wanted to see her.

But she was worried about the FBI tracking her, she told him. It was too soon.

He told her that she and the others should send more money, not only for him, but so they could all invest in a Jet-ski operation. He had talked to a Mexican lawyer about setting up a Jet-ski rental outfit. They would need about $80,000 to begin, and then they could live off the rental fees. "This company can send you-all a big check every month," he said.

Back in Charlotte between his trips to Mexico, McKinney occupied his evenings little differently from when he was in Cancun. He drank and met women in Charlotte's stylish hangouts—an Irish bar called Ri-Ra, a yuppie bar called Rockbottom, the South End Brewery, Cosmos, and Vinnie's Sardine Grill and Raw Bar. If it got late and he lacked female companionship, he sometimes headed to the Paper Doll Lounge, a strip joint. He usually returned to his hotel room in

Gastonia or Charlotte, where he waited to talk to Steve about his upcoming travels to Mexico. Before each trip, they agreed that McKinney would try to kill David if the circumstances were right. If they weren't, McKinney would continue to earn David's trust so he could get close to him—physically, in private—on future trips. Or he would try to arrange for David to move to another country, maybe Brazil.

One evening in early December, David was eating dinner at Cancun's Hard Rock Café while watching rock videos on the main dining-room screen and catching a glimpse of the beach. Another customer approached his table. "Hey, man," the stranger said, "you look like that guy from North Carolina who stole like $20 million."

Inside, David froze. "That's cool," he said. "But my name's Mike."

The stranger returned to his table, oblivious to David's worst panic attack since he had been in Mexico. He finished his meal in a daze, discretely paid his check, and went back to his apartment.

He paged Kelly. He got her on the phone and told her what just happened. "I gotta get out of here," he said.

She told him they would send Bruno back, that they would think of something. Steve would arrange to have him moved to Brazil or somewhere else, she said.

David began staying in his apartment all the time, scared he would be recognized. Then, a few days later, he decided to get a room at a Holiday Inn. Moving around would get potential reward seekers off his trail, he figured.

One day in mid-December, about a week before Christmas and just after the Hard Rock Café sighting, Bruno called David at the hotel. He said he had more money for David and that he was going to help him move.

The two met at the Clarion Inn Resort at Colinda Beach. Bruno told David about a plan to move him to Mexico City, and then maybe to Brazil.

Back in his rented apartment, David explained to Lindsey that he had to go to Cozumel for a few days. He took some clothes and the Ray-Ban sunglasses with him, leaving behind the expensive scuba equipment, a CD player, pots, pans, and about $15,000 in cash that he had stashed in the place.

Then he and Bruno took a forty-five-minute cab ride south on Route 307, a four-lane road with trees on each side, to the tamer resort area of Playa del Carmen, a former fishing town that had grown popular when nearby Cancun started entertaining tourists in the 1970s. On the ride, David asked in a quiet, shaky voice if Bruno knew who he was. Bruno said no, and that he could not care less.

When they arrived in Playa del Carmen, David and Bruno took a ferry to the resort island of Cozumel, known worldwide for its fantastic diving. They got a room at the plush, four-star Presidente Hotel, where rates started at about $310 a night. The room had a balcony. They went outside, sat down, and poured themselves drinks, looking down on the hotel pool. The tops of the palm trees in the hotel's garden reached their floor. In the distance, they could see Playa del Carmen. They started talking.

"I used to be a truckdriver," David said. "I'm doing pretty good for myself, huh?"

McKinney, who thought David was just an ordinary guy running from an ordinary shooting, nodded.

David then proceeded to tell him how, exactly, he wound up in Mexico. "I hit it for $14 million," David said.

As David told the story, McKinney noticed his voice fill with confidence. McKinney was impressed, yes, but he was also scared. He had thought this was about some rinky-dink killing over drugs that American detectives would never seriously consider investigating across the border.

The discussion turned to how Americans on the lam could make a living in Mexico. David brought up the Jet-ski business. With a $75,000 to $80,000 investment, they could buy eight to ten Jet-skis, he said.

Then they could rent them out for $80 or $90 an hour. There would be no need to ever return to America. Of course, David and McKinney were not going into business together. It was just small talk. They were both in Mexico for different reasons, and only one of them figured he had to stay.

McKinney mentioned that David's cohorts were spending the money wildly in North Carolina, moving into a fancy new home and buying high-end vehicles.

This news perturbed David, who felt that as the most essential team member, he should have the highest standard of living.

Until this point, McKinney had figured he was in little danger of getting arrested. He had not heard of the Loomis Fargo heist. But after hearing David describe it, he realized there was a pretty good chance that everybody involved would get caught. And he thought to himself that they weren't paying him enough. Still, he did not bail out of the plan, figuring that maybe, just maybe, he could arrange for someone else to do the deadly deed. Then McKinney would get his $250,000 from Steve and be on his merry way. He had recently hooked up with a local hoodlum named Robert, who worked a low-level job in Cancun's tourism industry. He had asked Robert if he knew anyone who would help McKinney kill somebody. Robert said he would help.

Now, talking at the hotel, Bruno told David he was going to fly to Mexico City himself to find a place there for David to temporarily stay before the move to Brazil. Meanwhile, he said, David should go back to Cancun and call Robert, who would get David a plane ticket to Mexico City.

David's love for the Pittsburgh Steelers probably saved his life.

He called Robert, a six-foot-three, three-hundred-pound brute. They arranged to meet at Señor Frog's waterfront bar in Playa del Carmen, where tourists sipped tropical drinks in eighteen-inch glasses.

Robert's attention was immediately drawn to David's Steelers jersey, which had the name and number of running back Jerome Bettis. "Man, where the hell did you get that jersey?" he asked. "I been looking all over for something like that!"

They made sports talk over Dos Equis and chips and salsa. David gave Robert about $200 worth of pesos to buy him a one-way ticket to Mexico City. Robert gave David a cell phone.

The next day, Robert called David to say the money had been stolen. "Come to Cancun to see me again," he said. "I'll put you up. I need to talk to you anyway."

David took a cab to Cancun and wound up meeting Robert's family. Everybody got along.

"Man, I feel bad about what's gonna happen to you," Robert said. He explained that Bruno had tried to get one of Robert's boys to kill David. "What'd you do?" he asked David.

"I'm a bank robber," David said.

"Man, you're in a bad way," Robert said. He said he liked David—the love of a common sports team making them feel closer than they were—and felt guilty about being a player in his planned killing. He told David that Bruno wanted to take him to a jungle or somewhere isolated and finish him off.

Robert did not know it, but Mike McKinney had in fact just hired somebody to kill David in Mexico City. Steve Chambers then surprisingly called off the murder, at least for the time being.

David was flabbergasted by Robert's words, and it showed on his face.

"What you really oughta do," Robert said, "is go right back to these people with a gun and kill them."

The suggestion did not erase David's look of shock. How was he going to kill anyone? True, he had been in the army, but he had worked repairing helicopters.

"Keep your distance from Bruno," Robert told him.

It was starting to make sense to David why the money was coming down in dribs and drabs. He felt he owed Robert for saving his life.

He gave him $3,000 because he was grateful. In return, Robert set David up with a fake Mexican ID and birth certificate.

David wondered who else could be in on it. He did not suspect Kelly, thinking she was just a middle person. It was probably her friend Steve, who seemed to control all the money, from what Bruno had said on the hotel balcony.

David called Kelly and asked if she still had the .45 caliber gun he left with her the night of the crime. He figured that with Steve around, she might need it.

And he figured he would not see his share of the money without a fight.

Parties in the Big House

WHILE DAVID GHANTT WORRIED in early December about getting his share of the loot in Mexico, Steve Chambers fretted in North Carolina over safeguarding the whole kit and caboodle.

This had become a serious problem. Amy Grigg's half-brother, Jody Calloway, and his wife, Jennifer, had seen a receipt from Lincoln Self Storage lying around the Grigg home and had schemed to steal from the facility. First, on November 22, 1997, Jennifer rented her own locker there, to gain access past the computer-keyboard security system. Jody practiced working with a torch. In late November, Jody burned Nathan Grant's locker open and stole about $1.3 million. It was the hottest money around, having been stolen twice in two months. Before he left, Jody replaced the damaged lock with a new, identical one.

Nathan Grant and Amy Grigg had collected about $70,000 from Steve to keep watch over the storage facilities. When Amy checked on one of the lockers and could not open it, she nervously told Nathan. A few days later, her fiancé checked it out himself. Amy was right, he discovered; the locker would not open.

They panicked. Nathan bought 3-In-One oil, hoping maybe the lock was frozen and needed something to loosen it up. He worried that if anything happened to the money, Steve would think he stole it. Amy, unaware that Jody had stolen the money, told her half-brother she had been hiding it for the mob, and that now she was scared "they" might come after her.

Two weeks later, on December 1, when Nathan tried again to open the locker, his key still did not work.

Later, his face white as a ghost, he told Steve. They drove together to the facility and looked closely at the locker. They saw burn marks, and Steve figured somebody probably had cut their lock off and replaced it with an identical one. He talked to a woman who worked at the storage facility, but she was not helpful. It was not her responsibility, she said. So Steve had her call a locksmith. When the locksmith cut the lock off, Steve opened the locker and found it was empty. Half a dozen suitcases and four cardboard boxes, all full of cash, were missing.

Nathan panicked.

Steve stayed calm. He did not curse or yell. He continued to lie to Nathan about the source of the money, saying he had been holding it for others. "They're gonna kill me," Steve said. "I gotta go to Chicago and explain to them that it's gone."

Of course, Steve could not report the theft to the cops. All he could do was try to keep the rest of his money in safer hands. First, he removed the money from the other storage lockers. Then he asked his relatives and friends to help him store it in safe-deposit boxes.

The loss would not put a rich man like Steve Chambers in the poorhouse. It would not even threaten his $8,860 monthly mortgage payments. He could still afford to buy his old mobile-home property, using a $62,000 check he secured for a fee through the father of Calvin

Hodge—the ice-cream man who in October secured a cashier's check for the $635,000 house. Steve then let Nathan and Amy live there, for $500 a month. And he could afford to pay his lawyer, Jeff Guller, a $10,000 fee for simply holding two briefcases in his office. The briefcases contained $433,000 that Steve planned to buy his new house with, before Guller told him that paying with cash required filling out forms. Guller, whose office assistants almost immediately worried the cash was Loomis Fargo money, was reluctant to take a fee for holding the money, but he relented when Steve, in the end, called it a Christmas gift.

After Thanksgiving, Steve asked for his briefcases back. Guller returned them on consecutive Sunday mornings, November 30 and December 7, in the parking lot of a fish camp—the Southern term for a restaurant that serves monstrous portions of fried fish—off New Hope Road in Gastonia, on Guller's way to go boating on Lake Wylie. When Guller returned the second briefcase, Steve asked if he had taken his $10,000. Guller said yes, he had.

It wasn't the only secret meeting of the month involving a cash exchange. Steve met his cousin Scott Grant, who had helped out the night of the theft, in a Wal-Mart parking lot to give him $6,000.

Michele loved her new white BMW Z-3 and drove it all around Gaston County. Out of everything bought so far, this was her favorite. One day, wearing a pair of overalls, she drove it to her parents' house.

"Shelley," her mom said, "this is a very expensive car. How can you afford this?"

Michele told her mother that she and Steve had leased it. Her mother decided to believe her, reasoning that it was easy to lease an expensive car that you could not afford to buy.

Steve and Michele hosted several parties and family events at which the man of the house conducted business and showed off his new wealth.

On December 12, they invited relatives over for Michele's daughter's sixth birthday party. Everybody ate from deli trays and cartons of Breyer's ice cream and marveled over the three-tiered castle-shaped cake. The party had a Cinderella theme.

During the party, Steve asked his father-in-law, Dennis Floyd, a truckdriver, to come downstairs with him. They played pool on Steve's $10,000 table and made small talk. Then they sat down at the basement bar. Steve said, "You know, we do a lot of gambling, and Michele tells me you're in a financial bind."

"If you drive a truck, you're always in a financial bind," Dennis Floyd replied.

Steve told his father-in-law he would give him $20,000 to "hold" $1 million. Dennis Floyd would need to sign up to manage a safe-deposit box—in his own name—in which Steve would hide cash.

Dennis Floyd said he was willing.

Days later, Michele drove her BMW to her parents' house in Mount Holly to pick up her stepfather. She had $1 million in a briefcase and wanted to take it to the bank.

She was wearing a silver raincoat. Her stepdad was wearing a black leather jacket. They were like Bonnie and Clyde, Michele thought. Michele pulled into a parking space at the bank. Lady and stepfather popped their doors open and walked to the trunk on opposite sides of the car.

Once inside the bank, they cosigned for access to a safe-deposit box.

In the coming weeks, Steve would pay his in-laws another $20,000 to open more safe-deposit boxes that would hold another $900,000 in "gambling money." In total, Dennis Floyd would rent seven boxes.

The Chamberses also asked Steve's parents to hide money and other things in safe-deposit boxes. His parents asked why. They told Steve's mother they had won at gambling in Las Vegas and told his father they had important papers and jewels that needed extra security. Steve's parents cosigned for three boxes. Steve said he would help them with a down payment for a new home.

Steve also got his friends in on the act. The best man at his wedding, David Craig, accepted $80,000 to open six safe-deposit boxes in his own name that would hold a total of $1.9 million in heist money. Steve said the money belonged to a friend who needed it shipped offshore. In addition, Calvin Hodge accepted $40,000 from Steve to open three safe-deposit boxes in his own name that would hold $900,000. He also rented a storage unit that hid $770,000.

Steve involved his cousin Nathan Grant as well, asking him to cosign for a safe-deposit box with Amy Grigg. About $400,000 went inside.

Despite the theft from Lincoln Self Storage, Steve still trusted his cousin. He occasionally cracked, "You owe me $1.96 million," but only as a joke. Nathan and Amy, worried that whoever Steve had been holding the money for would come after them, told Steve they were scared. Steve told them not to worry, that the people "up north" did not know Nathan and Amy were involved.

Nathan and Amy had just begun living with their year-old son in Steve and Michele's old mobile home. They used some of the $70,000 that Steve had given them to buy a tanning bed for $3,200, a computer for $5,000, a forty-eight-inch TV for $1,500, an engagement ring for $1,100, a washer and dryer for $1,300, and a Suzuki motorcycle.

In mid-December, Steve called an old friend with whom he had worked as a teenager at Belmont Hosiery, a sock factory. They had lost touch for about a decade afterward but reconnected in 1994 at a little-league game. Steve invited the friend, who now worked as a printing-company manager, to his New Year's Eve party.

The friend, who lived in Belmont, told him he thought the drive to Lincoln County would be too far, at least forty-five minutes.

"Don't worry," Steve said. "I moved."

"Where to?"

"I live in Cramer Mountain now."

"Get outta town!"

The friend drove to see Steve before the New Year's Eve party, in late December. The grand piano, the pool table, and the poker table all caught his eye. Steve said that the place cost more than $500,000, and that he had already paid off most of it.

"How the hell did you manage that?" the friend asked.

"It all comes from taking risks," Steve said.

"It looks like you're doing pretty good," the friend replied. "Can you get me hooked up?"

"I might have something for you," Steve said.

The friend asked for a loan for $25,000 at 1 percent interest. Steve said he would get back to him.

Kelly Campbell continued as a more-than-occasional guest at the Chambers mansion. Steve figured he had better keep a close eye on her before she did something stupid.

Of course, compared to Steve, Kelly was not spending much at all. She had bought the new minivan, leather jackets, an all-terrain vehicle, and dirt bikes and had just taken her kids to Disney World—the first time she had ever flown in a plane. She was more or less following Steve's advice from the night of the crime—that everyone lie low and hold off on big purchases. When acquaintances noticed she was spending more money, she explained that she was just selling pot.

She was still talking to David on the phone from Mexico every week or so. During a December call, she listened to him say he did not want to meet Bruno anymore. He would not say why, but he was insistent that somebody else make the cash deliveries.

When Kelly told him about her recent trip to Florida with the kids, he said he knew about the other purchases—the vehicles, the big house. He said he was not pleased, especially since he had seen less than $40,000 of the $17 million.

Kelly told David, "Yeah, that's what Steve is doing, but I haven't bought anything but a van."

Kelly did not complain to Steve about his extravagance. One day, Steve volunteered to her, "I know you're probably thinking, here I am buying all these things, when I told y'all not to. But I got ways to make it look legitimate."

Kelly did not argue with Steve. She took his word for it.

But she was increasingly nervous, since the FBI's interview with her at the Gaston Mall, that her connection to David would lead to her arrest. She figured Jeff Guller had not done all he could to make the agency leave her alone.

Steve referred her to another Gastonia attorney he knew. Kelly told this lawyer the FBI wanted to polygraph her. She paid the lawyer's firm $10,000 as a retainer. The lawyer set up a private lie-detector test administered by a retired FBI agent. Kelly failed it miserably.

Steve had hired this second lawyer for himself because he was upset with the plea bargain that Guller had arranged on his fraud case. Steve was considering buying a bar or a nightclub as a way to launder money, but he first needed his criminal record cleared of the charges, since the state would not grant a liquor license to a felon. Steve wanted both lawyers, separately, to explore having his guilty plea overturned.

Eric Payne was not renting any safe-deposit boxes, but he was still benefiting from his association with Steve. In November, he and a friend flew to a NASCAR race. In mid-December, Eric's wife, Amy, gave $12,000 in cash to a friend named David Oiler and asked him to use it toward a Harley-Davidson motorcycle for Eric. Amy Payne asked Oiler to title the motorcycle in his own name, which he did. Soon, she also got breast implants and a nose job, paying for both procedures with cash. Eric's two sisters also got breast implants. Eric bought a Chevrolet pickup truck from a dealership in Mount Holly for $31,000, putting

$6,000 down, trading in his old truck, and agreeing to make monthly payments of $357 for five years. For Christmas, he bought a diamond necklace for his wife and a computer for their daughter. He also bought a riding lawn mower.

Sandra and Dennis Floyd did not visit their daughter's new home often, but Sandra did have a hand in some of the decorations. She traveled with Michele to the Southern Christmas Show in Charlotte, where, in early December, they paid $600 for a six-foot-tall cigar-store Indian for inside the house. They drove back on Interstate 85 to Michele's home with the Indian sticking out of the hatchback because it would not fit inside. Other drivers stared at them like they were idiots.

Steve and Michele continued to sock money away in banks. On December 17, Michele walked into a Wachovia Bank in Gastonia and deposited $15,000 in cash. She also rented two safe-deposit boxes,

Steve and Michelle Chambers moved into this $635,000 house in a gated community in Cramerton, North Carolina, less than a month after the heist. The movers in the picture are taking away seized dining-room furniture after the couple's arrests.
Robert Lahser / CHARLOTTE OBSERVER

each of which measured ten inches by ten inches by twenty-one inches.

Husband and wife had been visiting several area banks once or twice a week since the heist, depositing a total of $26,521 in NationsBank and First Union in November and $54,460 in NationsBank, First Union, and Wachovia in December. On December 19, Michele carried a briefcase of cash into First Union and made a deposit of $6,408.

About a week later, they held a Christmas party at 503 Stuart Ridge. It was catered by the Boston Market restaurant chain—turkey, ham, and all the trimmings. The tree, about twelve feet high and trimmed to the hilt, stood impressively next to the curved staircase.

The most memorable part of the day was gift-giving time. Michele and Steve gave her grandfather Roy Willis a small, wrapped box. They made sure their video camera caught his reaction. He slowly opened the package, wondering what his newly rich granddaughter had bought him. Inside, he saw a small Matchbox pickup truck and a key. He was speechless. He realized what they were doing, that his gift was a real pickup, and that it was probably outside. He cried out of joy. He had always wanted a pickup truck. His reaction touched everyone.

Dennis Floyd was grateful when he received his gift, a 1978 Honda motorcycle.

But the next gift, for Michele, was even more astounding. Steve gave her a brown teddy bear. Michele opened the bear's zipper and saw her real gift—a three-and-a-half-carat diamond ring. She did not know it yet, but Steve had paid $43,000 for it. He bought it in Charlotte, at Southpark Mall, with a lot of cash. When the employee at Carlyle Jewelers had asked him for information to fill out the mandatory cash-reporting form, Steve provided a phony name and a made-up social security number.

Even during the best of times, criminal multimillionaires have a lot on their minds. Several potential problems troubled Steve. What would happen if David Ghantt decided to turn himself in? What if the murder plot went wrong? What was the best way to hide the money? He was nervous over these issues, but not so nervous that he felt he couldn't fish for information from the FBI. He placed a Christmas call to the bureau's Charlotte office.

He asked for Phil King, the agent he had worked with before, when he was an informant. He said he just wanted to say hello, to find out how King was doing. Steve asked King if he was working on any special cases lately. He hoped the answer would be a gauge to the FBI's progress on the heist investigation.

Just the usual stuff, King said.

Steve wished him a Merry Christmas and jokingly asked, "Did you buy me a gift?"

King returned the sentiment, and the joke. Then they hung up.

One day in early January 1998, Steve and Michele invited their friends for a night on the town. They even set up Kelly with a blind date, knowing she and her husband were having problems.

Steve rented a limousine. For dinner, they ate at a Charlotte steakhouse. Steve tipped the limo driver hundreds of dollars, giving him a twenty-dollar bill each time he opened the door.

After dinner, they went to a nearby nightclub called Crickets. Kelly and her date were not hitting it off. One sign of this was that her date was dancing quite closely with Michele. This perturbed Steve, whose reaction caused a scene at Crickets. The manager asked them to leave. While getting kicked out, Steve told the manager, in a huff, that he was going to come back one day soon and buy the place.

It was not a pipe dream. It would be Steve's biggest non-house purchase yet. The place was a dive with pool tables, a dance floor, and a bar, but Steve figured it might be the perfect way to launder money. He soon had a rough marketing plan. He would change its name to The Big House—as in prison—and the slogan would be, "If you're gonna do the time, do it right." He and Michele had visited a similar bar in upstate New York.

He talked with the owner and came up with a tentative purchase price of $450,000.

The club probably would not be Steve's only new venture. One day, at M&S Furniture, he told Ruth Staley, the mother of the previous owner, that he planned to open more businesses in the area—a cigar store, a cigarette store, and maybe something at Gastonia's old Franklin Hardware location.

"That would be nice for downtown," Ruth Staley replied.

Steve and Michele liked Ruth Staley. One Friday in late December, they asked her to bring her three grandchildren over to their house for pizza, saying they always bought pizza for their kids on Fridays to celebrate the end of the week.

Ruth accepted the invitation. The size of the house impressed her. During the visit, Ruth noticed the blue barrels in the garage. Ruth liked the barrels' royal blue color, and told Michele. "What do you have in those?" she asked.

"Dog food," Michele said.

Steve and his old friend from Belmont Hosiery continued talking. In the second week of January, Steve offered the friend $100,000 to smuggle $2.5 million to the Cayman Islands. A cruise ship was the best way to do it, Steve said.

Steve planned to protect his own interests. He told the friend he would plant another person on the ship to watch him, as insurance, to make sure he did not run away with the money.

The friend told Steve he would think about the deal and get back to him.

Jody and Jennifer Calloway needed to make a smooth getaway from

North Carolina with their approximately $1.3 million in twice-stolen money. Jennifer had family in Colorado, so they decided to move there. As part of their plan, each would tell the boss at work that the other one was being transferred. They would write almost identical resignation letters.

They were a physically attractive couple, he with dark hair and a handsome face, she with blond hair and a good figure.

Jody, twenty-eight, was a United States Air Force veteran who had worked two years at Pattons Inc., an air-compressor company. His hourly wage was $11.45. "Although I have been afforded a great opportunity with such an innovative company," Jody wrote his boss, "I am putting my two-week notice in. My wife has accepted a job outside of North Carolina which would be to our family's advantage. I am sad that I have to leave when I am just becoming fully proficient at my job. However, I would like to thank you for giving me the chance to work with and become part of a winning team."

Jennifer, a General Electric employee, wrote her boss, "Although I have been afforded a great opportunity to work with such an innovative company, I am putting my two-week notice in. My husband has accepted a job outside of North Carolina which would be to our family's advantage. I am sad that I have to leave when I am just becoming fully proficient at my job. However, I would like to thank you for giving me the chance to become part of a world-winning team. I am very proud to say that I have worked for GE. Since I have worked here I actually felt myself grow as an individual and professionally. I hope that one day our paths will cross again.

"Again, thank you," she finished, "for the invaluable experience of what a company should be."

Her last day was January 9, 1998. They moved to Littleton, Colorado, where they used their stolen cash to persuade a landlord to rent them a house even though they lacked employment. They accomplished this by paying, up front, their security deposit and six months of rent at $1,300 a month, for a total of $9,100.

The Calloways' house on West Berry Street in Littleton was nothing like Steve and Michele's Cramerton mansion, but it was a significant upgrade from their Carolina living arrangements. It had fourteen hundred square feet, a finished basement, and a two-car garage. They bought two vehicles—a blue Ford Explorer for $32,784 and a green year-old Chevy Tahoe for $23,982. Unlike their unwitting North Carolina benefactors, the Calloways took out five-year loans. They also paid $8,500 for a boat, just over half in cash and the rest with a money order.

A Careful David

HE WAS LONELY IN MEXICO and had nowhere else to go. His wife probably loathed the very thought of him. His new honey in North Carolina was stalling him. And now, his one physical contact with his team back home, the person actually delivering him money, was most likely trying to kill him.

Such was life for David Ghantt in January 1998. He began to wish he had never stolen the money. He still felt no remorse toward Loomis Fargo, but he sometimes wondered how much longer he would be alive. And he didn't know how much of the stolen money he would see, if he was lucky to remain alive. Calling the FBI with the truth about the heist and the hit man did not sound like such a horrible idea, or so he occasionally thought—but just occasionally.

Since Robert the mystery man had told David that Bruno was working to kill him, David's nerves had gone haywire. That chance sighting at the Hard Rock Café by someone who recognized David as the thief from North Carolina paled in comparison as a panic inducer.

David was now staying at hotels in Playa del Carmen. Its beaches lacked the beauty of Cancun's, but the odds seemed slimmer that he would be recognized. Still, he nervously looked over his shoulder as he walked the streets, wondering if Bruno was stalking him among the other pedestrians, or was in a car somewhere with a rifle and a scope. Two or three times a day when he walked the avenues, he cut through side alleys and turned his head to see if anybody was following him. If that did not reveal anything—and it never did—he would stop suddenly, turn around, and smoke a cigarette for two minutes, just to see if anybody else changed his path abruptly or looked as though he did not fit in. While getting his hair dyed one day, he overheard other men in the barbershop using the word *policia*. He did not hear the context. Still, he excused himself to go to the bathroom, left twenty dollars to pay, and bolted out the back of the shop with his hair half-dyed. He washed the brown out when he got back to his room.

At restaurants, he sat near the back, by the exit and the bathrooms, so he was always ready to slip away if he had to. At night, he kept the lights on. He often could not sleep, partially out of fear and partially because the lights were on. Some nights, he stayed up with a pot of coffee, worrying. Other nights, he drank Jack Daniel's, emptying a bottle by himself and passing out.

He did not know that Bruno was actually Mike McKinney, but he stopped using McKinney's name for himself anyway, out of concern he would be traced. Instead, he used the name James Kelly, because it was similar to John Kelly, a character he enjoyed from Tom Clancy's novel *Without Remorse*. He went by the name John Clark, also used in *Without Remorse*, at the El Tucan Hotel in Playa del Carmen. He even assumed the identity of a cartoon character, checking into one motel as George Jetson.

Cancun and Playa del Carmen attract so many couples and single people seeking and finding fun that just seeing them enjoy themselves can depress someone keeping a low profile, like David. He began to long for his wife. Married life with Tammy had not been terribly exciting, but it was safe and predictable. She had loved him. He had loved her. He thought back to how they had met at the Winn-Dixie, to how it ended the first time when she dumped him, to how their romance slowly rekindled through the mail while he was in the Persian Gulf. He even had a fond memory of how she lost the diamond engagement ring he gave her—down the toilet, by accident—and just wore the wedding band. Did she still wear it? Did she still love him? He didn't know. He doubted he would ever see her or talk to her again. The same was true regarding his parents. He wished he could find a way to let them know he was alive. He knew his mother was heartbroken, and probably depressed.

But he figured the FBI was watching his family closely. If he called Tammy or his parents, the feds would trace the contact. And as bad as he felt about leaving them, he did not want to risk capture himself, or to risk getting them in trouble.

Still, he was tempted. His life had been so simple with Tammy, especially after they married in 1992 and moved to Hilton Head to live with David's sister. David worked at an appliance store, then at the airport, helping fuel and direct planes on the runway. On weekends, they would walk along the beach and go to the arcade, where they would play Skee-Ball and video games. They moved back to Gastonia three years later and lived with her parents for six months, but then they rented a place of their own. Every Friday night, they would go out to eat, either to a fish camp, a Chinese restaurant, or a steakhouse.

In reality, though, David knew that there had been serious problems. He absolutely despised the forty-five-minute drive to Loomis Fargo, and he didn't get to see Tammy as much as a husband should see his wife. And she wanted kids. He was not sure fatherhood was for him.

For most of January, David stayed inside his hotel rooms, watching HBO and eating M&M's. He kept the TV on whenever HBO showed the movie *Men in Black*, starring Will Smith and Tommy Lee Jones. David watched it at least seven times. He also watched repeats of *GoldenEye*, the James Bond movie.

But Hollywood reruns proved mediocre companions. He was lonely, and upset at having spent Christmas alone a few weeks earlier, and terrified of Bruno, and depressed that he had given up his old life, which for all its flaws was seeming better each day.

If he saw Bruno again, it would have to be in a public place, he decided. But when he talked to him on the phone to arrange another cash delivery, Bruno said he wanted only a private meeting. That wasn't going to happen, David told him.

They met at a public place, a restaurant, but Bruno did not have any money for him. Bruno told David he had given the money to Robert, who would pass it along to him.

David met Robert, who again warned him not to see Bruno anywhere private. Robert also told David he was not going to be involved anymore. It was getting too dangerous, he felt.

It was late January the next time David and Bruno talked. David told him to leave the next cash delivery with a third party. David would get it from that person. That was the only way, David insisted.

Bruno said it sounded like David was trying to set him up.

"I don't give a damn about you. *Fuck* you," David said. And he hung up on Bruno, who realized Robert had probably blown his cover.

Bruno then spent the $10,000 he had brought for David. He would tell Steve the police in Dallas, Texas, had stopped him on his plane connection and taken it.

Of course, if he wanted his money, David remained at the mercy of his fellow thieves. In mid-February, he told Kelly, on the phone, about his argument with Bruno. He said he was considering turning himself in.

He booked a first-floor room at the Hotel La Tortuga, a quiet, just-opened inn that was only a two-minute walk from Avenida 5—Fifth Avenue—which was Playa del Carmen's popular pedestrian strip of bars, stores, mariachi bands, sellers of sliced melons, and restaurants like Apasionado—Spanish for "passionate"—which featured lobster soup, citrus-marinated shrimp, fried bananas with ice cream and chocolate sauce, and, on Wednesdays and Thursdays, flamenco dancers who hiked their flowing red-and-white dresses to their thighs, twirled their bodies, and rhythmically stomped their heels on the two-foot-high wooden platform.

David checked into the Hotel La Tortuga as James T. Kelly. The staff thought he was strange. He stayed alone in his room most of the time, reserving it day by day and paying with wads of cash he would remove, crumpled, from his pocket. He would place the money on the front desk and say, "Take out what you need for another night."

He stayed two stints at the hotel. Every day, the staff had to restock his room's mini-bar supply of M&M's—two new packs a day. The room was cooled by a ceiling fan. It had orange stone floors, wall paintings of two turtles—blue and green—a king-sized bed, a TV, and a whirlpool. It cost about $90 a night.

He persuaded Kelly to wire him $5,000. She used a Western Union in a Bi-Lo supermarket in Gastonia, wiring the money to the name of Mike McKinney. It would tide David over for a while.

But Kelly kept telling him to meet with Bruno, despite his concerns.

David wondered if she knew about this supposed murder plot. He still wanted her to come down to live with him, and he told her he loved her.

She did not commit.

David tried to add to her worries about staying in North Carolina. "I'll bet you money your phone's tapped right now," he told her.

Tammy was living with her parents just about full-time, trying to keep sane by taking her young niece to movies.

When David lived with her, they had spent different parts of Christmas at each other's parents' houses—Christmas Eve with her folks,

Christmas Day with his. Christmas 1997 was different. Two weeks before Christmas, Tammy visited David's family in Hendersonville, three hours away. When she got there, she found it depressing. She and David's relatives talked about him, wondering where he was, wondering if he was okay. They looked at pictures of him and told him to come home, as if he could hear.

Sometimes, through the grief, Tammy managed a happy memory. She thought of David's goofy sense of humor. He could do great impersonations of the cartoon characters Ren and Stimpy, and of Tim Allen from the TV show *Home Improvement*. He would sing the song of Barney the cartoon dinosaur for kicks, in a funny voice. He would give his nieces and nephews "wet Willies," sticking his finger, wet with saliva, into their ears for laughs. Before he would fart, he would ask someone to pull his finger.

Farting aside, David was a gentleman, Tammy thought. Not a thief. He would not desert his wife. Never. Somebody must have put him up to it, she still thought. After all, just before the theft, he had scheduled a follow-up dental appointment. Would he have done that if he meant to go away like this? It could not have been his idea.

Coming Together

An intriguing piece of information crossed FBI agent John Wydra's desk in early January. Record checks revealed that Kelly Campbell's new minivan was titled to herself and a man named Robert Dean Wilson. The name sounded familiar to Wydra. He checked it further, and it turned out that Robert Dean Wilson was an alias for Steven Eugene Chambers. It was one of the names he had used to scam money from banks.

The minivan alias seemed like the illicit connection the FBI was looking for. It seemingly tied Steve Chambers to Kelly Campbell, who agents had already comfortably tied to David Ghantt. But they needed to investigate further. After all, they could not prove the buyer was not a genuine Robert Dean Wilson.

The records showed Kelly's minivan was bought at the Harrelson Toyota dealership in Fort Mill, South Carolina. Wydra and another agent drove to the dealership to talk to the salesman who sold it. They showed him pictures of Kelly Campbell and Steve Chambers and asked if they were the two who bought the vehicle. The salesman said yes. He also said they paid for it entirely in twenties, bringing the money on two separate occasions. The agents already suspected a cash purchase, because records showed that no loan had been taken.

On January 12, as agents considered their next step, the FBI received a visit from Steve's old friend from Belmont Hosiery. He was accompanied by a lawyer and his uncle, who was a private investigator. The lawyer had contacted the FBI two days earlier, so the FBI already knew the reason for the visit.

Steve's old friend told Dick Womble, Mark Rozzi, and Vic O'Korn that he had been acquainted with Steve Chambers a long time ago, then had lost contact, but now was hanging out with him again. A few days earlier, Chambers had offered him $100,000 to take $2.5 million to the Cayman Islands. Wanting to do it, he had asked his uncle if anything seemed fishy or illegal about the deal. The uncle then called the lawyer, after which they contacted the FBI. The uncle told his nephew, after the call to the FBI, that the feds were all over Steve Chambers as a suspect in the Loomis heist, and that the nephew should talk to them. That's why he was here, Steve's old friend explained to Rozzi and Womble.

He said he had been suspicious about the source of Steve's wealth since he saw the house in Cramer Mountain. He told Rozzi that Steve had explained his riches with the line, "It all comes from taking risks." He also mentioned that Chambers invited him to a New Year's Eve party at his house, and that Kelly Campbell was there. He also spoke of Eric Payne, who Chambers had mentioned to him.

Rozzi told Steve's friend that the FBI already was on to Chambers, Kelly Campbell, and Eric Payne, but that the investigation was not yet complete. He asked the friend if he would consider helping the feds gather evidence by letting his phone conversations with Steve be taped.

The FBI wanted to see if Steve would admit involvement in the heist or blurt out anything about Ghantt. Rozzi explained that the FBI needed to find the stolen money and to locate David Ghantt, who many agents believed was dead. "We may have a murder on our hands," Rozzi said. "We've already heard what you've told us. But we haven't been able to get anybody inside this group."

Steve's old friend was nervous. He had a family and a steady job as a printing-company manager, and becoming an informant would be stressful and take time.

Rozzi told him the FBI would compensate him for any time he missed at work, if it came to that.

He said he would do it.

When they had first heard about Steve Chambers in November among the dozens of confidential tips about possible suspects, the FBI agents figured he might be involved in drugs, or gambling, or securities fraud, or a Ponzi scheme. He had a big house and big money, having made a big move despite lacking a legitimate source of income. But the newly discovered minivan purchase erased all doubt from the minds of Wydra and the other agents about Steve's heist involvement. Still, they would need to prove that involvement in court. In terms of evidence, it was far from clear that Steve and Michele Chambers had money from Loomis Fargo.

On a mid-January afternoon, Wydra secured some proof through physical surveillance.

The minivan connection had spurred the FBI to increase surveillance of Steve and Michele. Wydra and David Sousa, an Internal Revenue Service investigator, were waiting on January 16 at the First Gaston Bank in Mount Holly for Michele Chambers to come deposit money. She did not disappoint them, keeping to her practice of depositing on Mondays, Wednesdays, or Fridays, a schedule the FBI was aware of through bank records.

Wydra and Sousa were sitting in the branch manager's office when Michele walked inside, waited in line, and stepped up to the teller. She had $8,000 with her in a stack of bills with a little white wrapper around it. Wydra and Sousa watched the teller take the money, remove the wrapper, and throw it in the trash can next to her station. When Michele left the bank, Wydra and Sousa immediately walked to the teller. Luckily, the trash can was empty except for the wrapper. Wydra reached inside and saw that the wrapper had signed initials on it.

He took it back to his office. Upon checking with Loomis officials, he learned that the initials belonged to a Loomis employee who had counted money in the vault prior to October 4 but had been transferred to other duties afterward and had not since initialed money stacks. That meant not only that Steve and Michele were using money from Loomis Fargo, but also that it had come from the company on October 4, since none had been reported missing from earlier dates.

Many agents now felt the case was essentially solved. But there was division in the bureau. Some felt the time was ripe to make arrests. They had in their sights a couple who obviously had Loomis Fargo money and was spending hundreds of thousands of dollars of it. But others worried that making arrests without knowing the locations of Ghantt and the rest of the money would backfire. If the FBI arrested Chambers and Campbell while Ghantt or somebody else had the bulk of the money elsewhere, the feds might never recover it. And if Ghantt was dead and the FBI had no body or confession to prove it, the defendants could simply lie. And what if there was a plan among them to hide the bulk of the cash and keep mum if they got arrested? In addition, the FBI had no clear proof that Steve and Michele Chambers had actually helped Ghantt steal the Loomis money. Maybe other accomplices had passed the money on to them.

The evidence accumulated so far was too circumstantial to guarantee convictions, decided William Perry, who was in charge of the FBI's Charlotte office. He wanted the agents to wait until they found Ghantt and the money or proved that Ghantt was dead.

Charlotte's agents started working seven-day weeks again, and FBI surveillance experts flew in from New York and Atlanta to help.

The game plan involving Steve's old friend from Belmont Hosiery was to have him goad Chambers into talking about his involvement in the heist.

The first few recorded calls, placed January 18 and January 20, failed to do that.

Before he would do more, the printing-company manager had a request. He wanted agents Rozzi and Womble to talk with his wife. "I gotta tell you, she thinks I'm having an affair. She knows I'm not sleeping, and I'm making phone calls, meeting you guys out."

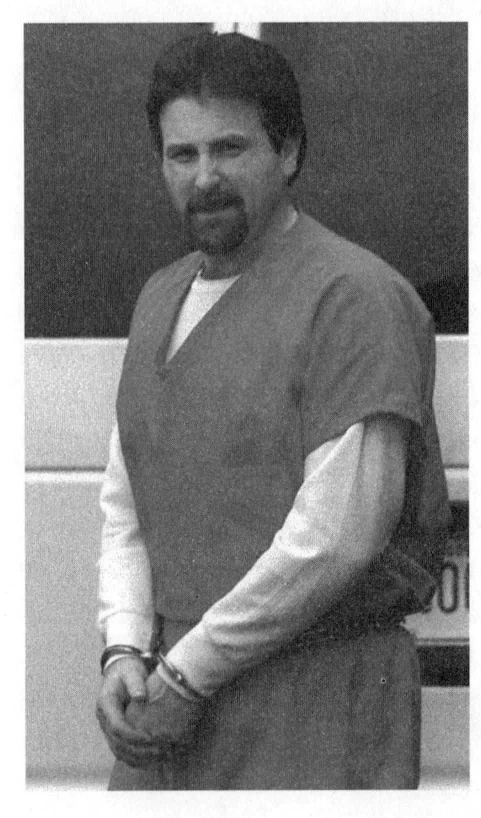

The FBI used physical surveillance and an active informant in their investigation of Steve Chambers.
CHARLOTTE OBSERVER

The surprised agents drove to their informant's house and explained the situation to his wife, who had known nothing. She asked Rozzi why her husband should bother getting involved. He answered that it could help the case, and that a large reward might result. She turned to her husband and said, "Baby, you can do this. I *know* you can."

Days later, doing what the FBI calls "tickling the wires," the printing-company manager called Chambers and said, "I'm hearing stuff around town that you had something to do with the Fargo heist."

"That's just Eric running his mouth," Steve said, referring to their mutual friend Eric Payne.

What the FBI really needed was to listen to Steve's phone conversations with other people. The confidential tips and the big house certainly made him out to be the lead beneficiary and money manager, but wiretaps were probably the only way to find out what was really happening.

Obtaining judicial permission to install wiretaps is an involved process. Eavesdropping on citizens' private phone conversations is about as intrusive as law enforcement gets. Judges require strong evidence from investigators that wiretaps will substantially help solve a crime, and that agents or detectives have already tried less intrusive methods.

The supervisors called in agent Erik Blowers, an expert at securing permission for electronic surveillance. Blowers, a former prosecutor in Columbus, Ohio, had experience in preparing affidavits to persuade judges to authorize phone surveillance. He could do it more quickly than anyone else in the bureau in Charlotte. He interviewed the agents involved, read their notes and documents, and wrote up the affidavit.

His affidavit said that investigative techniques short of wiretaps had not, and would not, get the FBI the evidence necessary to bring solid charges.

Blowers anticipated the judge's questions.

Why couldn't the FBI just keep using physical surveillance of the suspects? It wouldn't work, Blowers wrote, noting that the FBI had tried it on Campbell and Chambers, and that it was unlikely to solve the case. Why not? Because, Blowers wrote, Chambers had worked as an FBI informant in the past and was familiar with investigative techniques. He might be wary of surveillance. Furthermore, discretion would be especially difficult in the gated Cramer Mountain community.

Why not use undercover agents or additional confidential informants? It was true, Blowers wrote, that the FBI had used confidential informants to some success so far, but those informants were on the fringes of the criminal operation and were unable to provide needed evidence. And because of Steve's experience as an informant, he might be wary of anybody showing increased interest in his activities.

Why not interview the suspects or have them testify before a grand jury? This one seemed obvious to Blowers, but he preemptively answered it anyway. Anyone called to testify about a heist conspiracy could lie or invoke the Fifth Amendment, he wrote. Besides, issuing grand-jury subpoenas would alert suspects to the investigation and prod them to extra caution. They could flee or destroy evidence or threaten people they suspected were informants. Or they could tell Ghantt about the investigation and he could sever all ties, making his capture impossible. Moreover, if agents interviewed suspects outside the presence of a grand jury, they could clam up like Kelly Campbell had in October, Blowers wrote. Campbell had admitted to using drugs with Ghantt but denied knowledge of the heist. When pressed to take a polygraph, she stopped talking and told agents to speak to her attorney.

Why not just use search warrants? For the same reason they could not interview suspects, Blowers wrote. At this point, searches might yield little evidence. The suspects could have carefully hidden the money they were storing.

Telephone records solidified the FBI's case for wiretaps, as laid out in Blowers's affidavit. From toll records and pen registers, agents knew that Chambers was talking to other suspects on his home telephone. The records showed that between October 30, 1997, and January 24, 1998, ninety-eight calls were made between the Chambers and Campbell homes, forty-six between the Chambers home and Campbell's cell phone, and eight between the Chambers home and Eric Payne's cell phone.

Tax records from the Internal Revenue Service also helped. Between them, Steve and Michele had earned $17,296 in taxable income in 1995 and $24,007 in 1996. They should have barely been able to afford renting a single room in their house.

The FBI filed the request for wiretaps. On February 10, 1998, district-court judge Richard Voorhees approved them on two home telephone lines of Steve and Michele Chambers. The standard wiretap rules applied—if a conversation was not related to criminal activity, the agents had to stop listening and recording, at least for a while.

The wiretaps were quickly put in place, and the FBI was ready to listen. Agent Ray Duda coordinated a team of Mecklenburg County sheriff's deputies, Charlotte-Mecklenburg police officers, and FBI agents to man the phone lines twenty-four hours a day on the tenth floor of the Wachovia Building, in a gray-carpeted room equipped with recording equipment.

The FBI was doing a fine job keeping news of Steve and Michele's activity from the local media. Reporters did not know money was being spent so close to home. Some had heard off the record around the federal courthouse that Ghantt would soon be arrested. Gary German, the media tipster, called the *Charlotte Observer* once or twice in early February to say he had heard a rumor the Loomis Fargo case was "coming down" and that the feds had found Ghantt—"They're on to the motherfucker!"—but he knew no details about accomplices pumping the stolen money into the local economy. Calls to the FBI produced responses of "We're still investigating" and nothing else.

Indeed, as time passed without an arrest, those in the newsroom at the *Observer* assumed that Ghantt and anybody who helped him had left the area. Some editors, jokingly admiring Ghantt's guts, figured he might go down in history as the man who had gotten away with stealing the most cash ever.

Taking Care of Business

STEVE CHAMBERS LOVED MOB MOVIES, but he ignored an important lesson from one of the best of them, *Goodfellas.*

Henry Hill, a mobster played by Ray Liotta, laid it out. "Paulie hated phones," Liotta's character said, referring to New York crime boss Paulie Cicero. "He wouldn't have one in his house. He used to get all his calls secondhand. Then he'd have to call the people back from an outside phone."

That was so the FBI could not listen in on a personal line. But four months after the heist, Steve figured the feds did not know about him. On his telephone, he talked about big expenditures, about laundering money through the Gastonia nightclub he planned to purchase, and even about hiring a bodyguard—with all the money around, he figured he needed one.

For Christmas 1997, Steve had given his wife a three-and-a-half-carat ring costing $43,000. Less than two months later, on February 15, 1998, the day after Valentine's, he wanted to spend a bundle on her again. He called Reid's Jewelry Store in the Gaston Mall and asked how much its most expensive lady's Rolex watch cost. The salesperson said it went for $150,000. The rich man was humbled. He told the salesperson that he hadn't spent that much for his own watch for that, he paid $6,500—and that he wasn't going to spend that much for his wife's. He wound up buying Michele a $3,500 Rolex.

Later in the day, Steve took a call from Kelly Campbell, who recently had told him she was considering getting liposuction for her buttocks. She now told Steve she needed twenty grand. He said she should come over at seven-thirty that night to get it. Steve also suggested that Kelly leave her kids with her husband and move to a different state until the FBI left her alone for a while. But she said she wanted to stay with her family.

That same day, Michele made a call about expensive interior decorating and renovations to their house. She also called her sister to brag about her $43,000 ring.

While out and about later in the day, she called Steve, who told her about Kelly's liposuction plans. They laughed.

A man with his wealth needed protection. At the very least, having a bodyguard would be cool. Even better, he could get two bodyguards. From his home, Steve called a personal security company on February 16 and asked the woman answering the phone about hiring two full-time bodyguards. He owned a corporation, nightclubs, and a furniture store, he told the woman. He hung up without finalizing anything.

Later in the day, Steve talked to his cousin Scott Grant on the phone. Almost five months after helping with the theft, Scott was still nervous about getting arrested. Steve told him not to worry. "Nobody is watching," Steve told him. "The heat is off." Steve had given Scott only about $25,000 in heist money. He asked if Scott was broke.

Not yet, Scott said. But it wouldn't be long.

Steve told him to come work at the furniture store. Steve would verify his employment with any finance company that asked. Things were going so well, he told Scott, that he was thinking about buying the Crickets nightclub in Gastonia.

Full-time, professional bodyguards were expensive. So Steve figured he would pay Mike McKinney, the hopeful hit man and former marine, $400 a week for a lesser degree of protection. He talked to Mike on the phone on February 17 and said he wanted to discuss a security arrangement. Steve said he would find McKinney an apartment. He proposed the $400 salary and said McKinney would need to be careful.

McKinney said he could do it.

Steve told him that Kelly Campbell would bring him money the next morning.

Security was not Steve's only concern. He needed to convert more of his cash to certified checks or money orders for the Crickets nightclub deal, which called for $250,000 in checks plus $200,000 in cash. That day, February 17, he talked with Mike Goodman, one of the friends he had paid to acquire checks in October to help buy his house. Steve now wanted another certified check for $200,000, and he would pay Goodman 20 percent, or $40,000, as a fee. Steve said the money was in twenties, and that he wanted a check just like last time—through Goodman's wife, Kim, a bank teller. He would need the check in a week.

Kim told her husband to tell Steve that he and Michele should come to the bank when it was not busy, and that this time, they should not bring the cash in a briefcase.

About the same time, Steve was working with his old friend and check man Calvin Hodge on a backup plan. On February 18, they talked about Steve's getting $250,000 worth of checks in exchange for cash. Steve asked Calvin if he had talked to his old man.

Calvin said his father wanted a fee of 25 percent to 50 percent of the total.

They talked again the next day, and Steve offered $35,000 as a fee.

Steve wanted to go through with the Crickets purchase despite a potential problem. The law forbade someone with a felony conviction to get a liquor license, and Steve had pleaded guilty only three months earlier to those forty-two counts of obtaining property by false pretense. As things were, he could not get a liquor license. What he needed was some way to get his convictions pardoned.

Enter lawyer Jeff Guller. Guller knew an attorney who was noted for his skill at working with government officials to help people get pardoned for crimes.

Steve said he was willing to pay $10,000 or $20,000 in up-front money, a sort of good-faith deposit, and that he ultimately would pay as much as $250,000 for the pardon. Guller knew that was more than the going rate but figured that if Steve would pay $250,000 for a pardon, then who was he to suggest otherwise?

In the midst of his domestic money laundering, Steve was trying to have David Ghantt killed in Mexico. Failing that, he wanted to at least keep David happy enough that he wouldn't turn himself in. Steve still had never actually talked with Ghantt; that remained Kelly's task.

On February 20, Kelly—who also was considering a tummy tuck—called Steve from Myrtle Beach, South Carolina, where she was on vacation. She talked about David without using his name, telling Steve she had talked with him and that he was considering moving up the coast of Mexico, and that nobody spoke English where he was.

Steve also learned from Kelly that David apparently was nervous about dealing with Mike McKinney, who David knew only as Bruno. They were going to have to send somebody else to make the next cash delivery, and it had to be soon, Kelly told Steve.

Kelly said David was supposed to call her again in two days, at seven at night on a pay phone at Nichols Food Store on Wilkinson Boulevard in Charlotte. They planned to discuss David's next move. David would also give Kelly a new contact number.

It would be an important call, as far as Steve was concerned. He told Kelly to phone him with David's new location as soon as the call from Mexico was done. Steve planned to give David's location to McKinney.

But Kelly missed David's international call.

On February 22, the pay phone at the convenience store rang at 7:17 P.M. A man answered it. David said he had the wrong number and hung up.

The phone rang again at 7:23. No one answered it.

It rang at 7:29. Again, a man standing nearby picked it up.

"Who is it?" David asked.

"I'm just standing here, and I picked up the phone, man," the answerer said.

"Thank you very much," David said. And he hung up. Where was Kelly? He had no clue. Her absence made him nervous.

It turned out that Kelly was too tired to drive from her home to the convenience store. And David was not the only one miffed at her. Steve was furious when she told him later that night that she hadn't gone to take David's call, and that it was because she was sleepy. He tried to impress on her that he needed David's location so he could send his people to Mexico.

Twenty minutes later, David paged Kelly with information about their next telephone contact.

Kelly called Steve again, saying she had a pager message from David that he would call her tomorrow, February 23, at four in the afternoon. The pager message was 223984009898143—February 23, 1998, four o'clock, on phone number 9898 (the last four digits of the phone at the convenience store). Of course, the 143 meant "I love you."

Steve told her to call him after she talked to David. He was planning to send McKinney to Mexico on February 24.

This time—on Monday, February 23—Kelly was present and alert for David's call. He said he was near Cozumel, a resort island just off Mexico's Yucatan Peninsula.

"Coza-who?" Kelly asked.

"Cozumel," David said. "Cozumel."

Actually, David was lying. He was really in Playa del Carmen, near Cozumel, but he did not want to reveal his whereabouts. And he still did not want to deal with Bruno.

Kelly told him that somebody would visit him with more cash at five in the afternoon either the following day or the day after that.

David gave her an answering-service number that the person making the delivery was supposed to call after arriving. In the meantime, David said, he would be staying at a hotel in a rural location. David wanted money, but he also wanted love. From Kelly. They talked again about the possibility of her coming down to visit him.

Kelly couldn't come up with a solid excuse. She told him she wasn't sure anymore that life abroad was for her. She used to think money would make her happy, she said, but now she was not so sure.

She didn't say she would never move down, but David was worried. Was she backing out of the plan?

Before they hung up, they expressed love for each other.

On his end, David was confused.

On her end, Kelly immediately called Steve and told him David's location and contact number. She mentioned that David did not want to deal with McKinney anymore. They discussed killing him by injecting him with bleach. Steve suggested that Kelly travel to Mexico to draw David out for the killer. Maybe she could make love to him, and somebody else could inject him with Clorox.

Steve hung up with Kelly and called Mike McKinney. He told McKinney that David was in the Cozumel area and reminded him that David did not want to deal with him anymore. "He's absolutely saying he don't want you to come back down there," Steve said. "So the only thing I'm wondering is, how are you gonna get close to him if he's that damn far up that rural place where he can see you coming?"

"It all depends where he's at," McKinney said. "Unless we send somebody—a decoy—down there, and I can shadow him."

The decoy idea sounded good to Steve. "You might need to call and cancel that reservation for in the morning and let [me] see if we can get somebody down there who can pull him out. That's the only damn thing I know to do, 'cause he'll see you coming from a mile away now, if he's already seen you. He'll see you coming from a way, either way. I don't guess there's a way you can get hold of a rifle or any damn thing?"

"I probably could," McKinney said. "But it'd take me forever to get it."

"If he won't take nothing from you, I don't know how else you can get close enough to him," Steve said. "You know what I'm saying?"

"Well, there's ways," McKinney said.

"I don't want you going in there and trying to do it and you not being able to do it," Steve said. "You know what I'm saying?"

"Yeah," McKinney said.

"That might fuck up the whole situation all the way around," Steve said. "Like I said, just hang tight until the morning, and I'll call and let you know what I find out. . . . I'll know if we can get this person to pull him out and, you know, get close to him or whatever, and then that way give you a chance to get close to him and do it that way."

The next day, Tuesday, February 24, Steve worked the phones some more. He called his cousin Nathan. Nathan was not home, but Steve told Amy he had a job for him, for some quick money. Steve added that they might have to start talking on pay phones.

When Nathan called back, Steve told him he wanted him to travel to Mexico in the next few days to bring $20,000 to someone. He said he would pay Nathan $1,000. Nathan agreed. They hung up.

Later in the day, from her mobile home, Kelly called Steve's house.

They talked about delivering money to Ghantt. They would try to have it done two days later, on Thursday, February 26, they agreed.

Steve called McKinney and said he would come visit him in his hotel room the next day to talk about everything that McKinney needed to do on his next Mexico trip, which Steve told him would be Thursday.

Steve called McKinney on Wednesday with yet another change of plans. Nathan would not be ready to go on time. McKinney and Nathan would now leave for Mexico on Friday, February 27, instead of on Thursday. Steve told McKinney to make reservations for Friday morning for two people, himself and Nathan, whose passenger name would be Tommy Grant, his full name being Thomas Nathan Grant.

On Sunday, March 1, Steve called Nathan to his house and gave him $24,000 in cash. He told Nathan to give half to his traveling partner the next morning. When they arrived in Mexico, they should, between them, give $20,000 to the recipient. Both Nathan and his traveling partner were to keep $2,000 themselves.

Nathan took the money to his home and stashed it under a couch.

Even in the midst of a murder plot, Steve's mind was on other things. After all, what good was having David Ghantt dead unless Steve could manage his money? He was wheeling and dealing, or at least trying to. His efforts were taking him down paths from Gastonia to Raleigh to Mexico City.

In Gastonia, Mike Staley wanted more money for his furniture store than the $25,000 Steve had given him. Staley was dropping hints that he would be difficult if Steve didn't make him happy. Having been inside Steve's house and seen a bag filled with cash, he suspected Steve was involved in the Loomis Fargo heist. One day, after accusing Steve of stalling on the payments he expected, Staley looked straight at Steve and said, "I hope you burned your clothes." Steve stared back and said nothing.

Steve did not want to piss anybody off who might tell the authorities to look into him. He asked his lawyer to prepare a note saying he owed Staley $20,000 more. "I need a little agreement drawn up," Steve told Jeff Guller over the phone on February 24. He asked Guller to put together a promissory note that said he would pay Staley five grand the next day, and another five grand every four months for a year. "It's just more or less a little mumbo jumbo shit between us," Steve told Guller. "Staley knows he's going to be paid cash to him any damn way, so he ain't going to fuck around and say too much about nothing."

"Yeah," Guller said.

"Just every four months, the first of the month, he wants, you know, five grand."

"Okay," Guller said. He asked Steve what the money was for.

"It's just an agreement between me and him about something he's done for me, you know what I'm saying?"

This $600 piece greeted visitors in the basement of Steve and Michelle's new house.
CHARLOTTE OBSERVER

"Okay."

"Something kind of under the table," Steve said.

"Gotcha," Guller said. "So I'll just put 'For services rendered.' " Even if that lacked detail, it still put the transaction on the table, Guller figured.

The conversation then turned to the nightclub Steve was thinking about buying.

"I pursued this thing about the pardon some more," Guller said, bringing up Steve's hope of being able to buy Crickets. It would take between six and eight months to get the pardon, Guller said, because Steve's convictions were only four months old. And the $10,000 or $20,000 required up front would not buy 100 percent assurance that the pardon would actually come through. "I have made the inquiries, and I have kind of stayed after them," Guller said. "I've gotten it going as far as I can get it going for right now without now starting to put some money toward it."

Steve saw the transaction as a bribe. He trusted Guller when the attorney said the deal maker would get the pardon, but he was still a little worried. "I just don't want this shit stuffed in somebody's damn pocket," he said.

"No," Guller said. "Not at all. See, I'm getting involved with it to make sure things are going on."

Steve asked what it would cost him.

"You said, 'I'm willing to spend $250,000' on Friday," Guller said. "And certainly, I don't want it to cost that much. . . . I want to keep it under $100,000 if I can, but, you know, I don't know."

"Right," Steve said.

"I'm not even telling anybody you're willing to go that high," Guller said. "I want them to come back to me and say, 'Okay, we need ten here, ten there, and ten there.' Fine. But I'm not even willing to say you are willing to go to any more than that."

Steve asked Guller when he needed the first payment.

"Yesterday," Guller said. "Just whenever."

Steve said he would try to get it to him the next day.

There was more business to discuss during this February 24 call. Kelly needed help getting her husband, Jimmy, a new place to live. Problems had resurfaced in their troubled marriage, and Jimmy was going to move out. Steve wanted to make sure the property they bought for him was under a fictitious name. Guller was the man to make that happen, he figured.

Guller said he would try to help.

Steve began a strange negotiating process. "What do you charge for that, like a grand?"

"Yeah," Guller said.

"Do you want to charge more? Because she's paying," Steve said.

"That will work."

"You tell me. You tell me a price," Steve said.

"Make it $1,250," Guller said.

"I was looking more around $1,500."

"Deal," Guller said.

Steve and his attorney also briefly considered going into the illegal cigar business. Guller said he knew someone based in Mexico City from whom they could buy Cuban cigars. Each box held about twenty-five cigars. They could buy them for about $525 a box and then sell them. They could start with ten boxes and see how it worked.

They acknowledged up front that they were not sure this business would pan out.

Cuban cigars could be hard to sell in the United States, Guller said. "I don't think that we can get a good retail market," he said. "You can't advertise because it's illegal to have them."

"You know," Steve said, "it's an $8,000 fine on every cigar."

"Is that right?" Guller asked.

"It's $8,000 for every one that comes out of Mexico, you know. Everything that comes out of Cuba, it's an $8,000 cigar if they catch you."

"Goddamn," Guller said.

“That’s what I said, too,” Steve said. “Ain’t no cigar worth that much.”

Before the pardon could be arranged, Steve decided to back out of the Crickets deal. Guller advised him that keeping the required alcohol records for the state would be burdensome. Steve had paid the nightclub owner $100,000 as a deposit but requested it back, using the excuse that someone from the Internal Revenue Service was asking him about the deal. Steve received his money back.

The Final Touches

David Ghantt was probably still alive. To the FBI, that was the wiretaps' most important revelation.

The agents had done a lot of listening since Judge Voorhees let them secretly record Steve's phone calls beginning February 11. The first clue that Ghantt was alive came on February 20, a Friday, when agents recorded a call between Steve Chambers and Kelly Campbell. In it, nobody mentioned Ghantt by name. Campbell said she had talked to him, and that he said he was going to move up the coast, and that nobody spoke English where he was now. Campbell said they would need to send someone else to "make the drop" to him in the near future. She said he would call at seven o'clock Sunday night at a pay telephone at Nichols Food Store to say where he was. Chambers asked Campbell to find out, when he called, how much money he needed.

Most of the other calls the agents listened to showed that Chambers was spending money like there was no tomorrow. They heard about the $43,000 diamond ring. They heard he was considering buying a Rolex and hiring a bodyguard. They heard him discuss money laundering and buying the Crickets nightclub.

Unfortunately, Chambers never said anything on the phone that unmistakably incriminated him in the Loomis Fargo heist or gave agents any clue where the money was.

On February 21, Chambers listened as his friend Eric Payne told him, "People are talking." Payne said Chambers should beat up whoever was spreading rumors that they were involved in the heist.

Agents also listened to a recording that almost stopped their hearts. The Charlotte-Mecklenburg Police left a message on Steve's answering machine telling him there was a warrant for his arrest involving a worthless check—a check unrelated to the heist, the FBI knew. The police left a number to call. The FBI listeners acted fast. They called a Charlotte police supervisor and asked that the officers lay off the worthless-check charge for a while, because of more pressing matters. The supervisor agreed.

It sure seemed like Campbell and Chambers were talking about David Ghantt, but the FBI wanted to be certain.

Erik Blowers, the agent who had prepared the paperwork for the FBI's first wiretap application two weeks earlier, prepared another one for February 20. This application asked permission to secretly record calls at pay phones outside Nichols Food Store. It was the same paper-intensive exercise he had gone through earlier in the month. First, Blowers explained all the accumulated evidence against Ghantt, Chambers, Campbell, and Eric Payne. Then he cut to the chase—given the most recent conversation between Steve Chambers and Kelly Campbell, listening to the calls outside the store at seven o'clock on February 22 could be the only way to learn where Ghantt was. It was still too early to swoop in with search warrants, Blowers wrote, because they would not necessarily lead agents to all the stolen money, and because others involved in the heist would be alerted and alter their criminal behavior. "Physical surveillance of Kelly Jane Campbell on February 22, 1998, at 7:00 (A.M. or P.M.) without the requested interceptions will not conclusively implicate her in the above-delineated criminal activities even if she does receive a telephone call at Nichols Food Store," Blowers wrote.

Federal judge Graham Mullen gave the feds permission to tap the phones to hear Ghantt call Campbell.

To be on the safe side, the FBI also sent undercover agents to Nichols at both seven in the morning and seven in the evening on February 22, when the unnamed "he" was supposed to call. Nichols was a convenience store located behind a gas station next to the Catawba Mobile Home Park on Wilkinson Boulevard in Charlotte.

The call didn't come through at seven in the morning.

That evening was soggy. Two agents with cameras sat in a car outside, ready to snap away into the rearview mirror to catch an image of Campbell on the pay phone. Three other agents sat at a table inside the convenience store. Seven o'clock came and went. There was no sign of Kelly Campbell. Five after seven. Still nothing. Ten after seven. Nobody.

At 7:17, a pay phone outside the store rang. Campbell was not there to pick it up. The undercover agents stood by as phone surveillance machines monitored by their colleagues traced the call to somewhere in Mexico. Did that mean David Ghantt was in Mexico? There was no way to know, because when agent Brian Roepe picked up the phone and said hello, the man on the other end said, "I have the wrong number," and hung up.

The phone rang again at 7:23. Kelly Campbell still was not around. The ringing stopped.

It started again at 7:29. Roepe answered.

"Who is it?" the caller asked.

"I'm just standing here, and I picked up the phone, man," Roepe said.

"Thank you very much," the caller said, and hung up.

It had to be Ghantt. That was the consensus around the FBI office, and it was strengthened by a call recorded that evening between Steve Chambers and Kelly Campbell. Chambers wanted to know if Campbell had talked to their caller as expected. She said she had been too tired to drive to the pay phone. Chambers got upset, saying he needed to know where the caller was, so he could send his people "down there."

Then, twenty minutes later, apparently after getting paged by Ghantt, Campbell called Chambers back and told him that another call would come through at four the next afternoon. Chambers told Campbell to call him after the conversation.

The next day, Monday, February 23, the FBI recorded the phone call between Campbell and a man agents now *knew* was David Ghantt. An undercover agent snapped a picture of Kelly talking on the phone outside Nichols Food Store. In the conversation, David Ghantt said he was around Cozumel, Mexico, and gave Kelly a phone number for the money deliverer to call when he got there. The agents heard Ghantt tell Campbell he loved her, confirming their suspicion of a romance between the two.

But her ensuing call to Chambers and other calls the FBI heard on Tuesday, February 24, between Chambers and Mike McKinney were alarming. Mixed in with the discussion of apparent bribes, cigar smuggling, and money laundering was talk of rifles, human decoys, and "getting close" to somebody. They realized Ghantt's co-conspirators were trying to kill him. Kelly Campbell was giving information to Chambers about Ghantt's whereabouts, which Chambers was using to plot Ghantt's death. It seemed the scheme involved cash deliveries, but it was unclear to agents why Chambers would give money to a man he was trying to kill, unless it was to keep him happy temporarily.

Knowing about the murder plot changed everything for the FBI. Recovering the money became a lesser priority than saving Ghantt's life. Now, the agents had to find him and take him into custody before somebody killed him.

Ghantt had said he was near Cozumel, but the FBI did not know exactly where. The Mexican phone company was unable to provide precise information about David's last call.

Using another approach, the FBI told Steve's old friend from Belmont Hosiery to try to get Chambers to use him to visit Ghantt in Mexico. The agents advised the friend to bad-mouth McKinney, to get Chambers angry at him so he would send the friend instead. The friend set up a golf date with Chambers to discuss matters, but it rained, so they canceled. They said they would reschedule.

The FBI supervisors got a table at a restaurant called The French Quarter in downtown Charlotte, just around the corner from headquarters, to discuss their next step over dinner. Vic O'Korn and Rick Shaffer wanted to send four of their agents to Mexico to find Ghantt. O'Korn wanted to send SWAT-trained agents, at least one of whom

Upon learning David Ghantt was in Mexico, the FBI mobilized to have him arrested.
T. Ortega Gaines / CHARLOTTE OBSERVER

could speak Spanish. The FBI first needed clearance from the Mexican authorities, because the United States cannot send police officers or FBI agents abroad without permission of the other country. The request was made through the FBI's representative in Mexico City on February 24.

The Mexicans responded quickly—that night—and their answer was not to the FBI's liking. The feds could send a single agent, and he had to be unarmed. That agent could accompany armed officers with Interpol, the international police agency that links police departments worldwide and that, in Mexico, was composed of select Mexico City officers.

The supervisors decided to send Mark Rozzi, one of the first agents to respond to the theft almost five months earlier. Rozzi left on a US Airways flight the next morning. When his plane landed in Mexico City, five Interpol officers met him at the airport and escorted him to a private police plane. They flew to Cozumel, where they thought Ghantt was hiding, and checked into hotel rooms.

The water and the beaches beckoned, but Rozzi had come to work. He and the Mexican officers worked with phone-company officials to try to trace Ghantt's previous calls, but the phone company had not done a good job of recording the information. Rozzi maintained that the calls should have come from a Cozumel number, because that's where Ghantt said he was. But the company could not trace them.

While they waited for the phone company to come through, Rozzi and the officers tried the simplest approach possible—cold searches through Cozumel to find Ghantt. They split into two groups of three officers each and asked people if they had seen a tall, thin, red-headed white guy. Normally, someone fitting that description would stand out in Cozumel, but this was the heart of the winter festival season, so there were ten times as many people as normal. The officers talked to drunks and prostitutes, to bartenders and local residents. More than a dozen people said they *thought* they knew him. But they did not help the cause. They said things like "He's staying in that hotel over there with a prostitute" or "Yeah, he drinks in that bar across the street."

They probably didn't have the right man. All the leads died.

Back in North Carolina, the agents were recording more calls. They learned that Chambers was continuing to relay Ghantt-related information from Kelly Campbell to McKinney.

On February 25, upon learning that Chambers was supposed to visit McKinney at his hotel room, the FBI decided to apply for permission for microphone surveillance of room 403 of the Hampton Inn in Gastonia. At the time, Judge Graham Mullen was at a flower show at Charlotte's Merchandise Mart on Independence Boulevard, and agents Erik Blowers and John Wydra, accompanied by prosecutor David Keesler, drove to meet him there. Sheriff's deputies escorted them to a private room. Mullen granted them permission.

On Thursday, February 26, the agents listened to McKinney as he talked about making airline reservations to Mexico for himself and a man named Tommy Grant.

Meanwhile, they heard Chambers tell Kelly Campbell, on the telephone, that "the guys" would be leaving the next morning and should arrive in Mexico at about six-thirty that night. Then Chambers called McKinney to remind him to be on time at the airport early Friday, so he wouldn't miss the flight.

Then there was a glitch. Tommy Grant did not have his traveling papers in order and needed some time. Chambers was pissed off. He called McKinney to delay the trip three days, until Monday, March 2, so Grant could get a certified copy of his birth certificate.

The FBI also intercepted an electronic message to Kelly's pager, apparently from Ghantt. The message contained the following number sequence: 227983009898143. Cross-matching that with phone numbers, the agents took the message to mean that on February 27, 1998, at three o'clock, Ghantt would call Campbell at the phone outside Nichols Food Store. The 143, of course, meant "I love you."

Dick Womble had an afternoon shift of manning the microphone in the hotel room next to McKinney's. He could tell that McKinney was by himself. All Womble could hear through the wall was the sound of the suspect watching TV, drinking a lot of booze, and then pissing like a racehorse; one time, McKinney kept it going for almost the length of two commercials. With a chuckle, Womble realized he had experienced finer moments as an investigator.

At 9:20 A.M. the next day, Friday, February 27, another agent was manning the microphone when Chambers arrived in McKinney's room. For the next thirty-eight minutes, the two talked about plans to murder Ghantt with a gun and how they would conceal it. "If it fucks up," Chambers said, "we are all in a world of shit."

The recordings were solid evidence of a murder plot.

Sure enough, Ghantt called Campbell at three in the afternoon on Friday, February 27. The agents listened to him complain that nobody had arrived to give him money. Campbell, who had not yet heard from Chambers that the trip was delayed until Monday, said that someone would be in touch that day. Ghantt gave his phone number as 314-84, in room 101. Campbell said she would try to learn more details of the delivery. Ghantt said he would call back.

This time, quick database research was able to trace the call to the Hotel La Tortuga in Playa del Carmen. Bingo. The agents now knew exactly where Ghantt was.

They continued to monitor the phones, listening ten minutes later when Ghantt called Campbell back. She had no new information for him. They could sense his frustration. At the same time, their concern for Ghantt's life didn't stop the agents from chuckling among themselves when Campbell responded to his "I love you" with a halfhearted "I'm still gonna try to come down there."

Later that day, they heard Steve tell Kelly over the phone that the Mexican trip had been postponed again, this time until Monday, March 2.

Supervisor Rick Shaffer contacted Rozzi with Ghantt's location. Rozzi told his Interpol hosts.

Two undercover Interpol officers—a man and a woman—checked into the Hotel La Tortuga pretending to be a married couple. After learning the hotel's layout, they told Rozzi he would stand out, thanks to his bushy American mustache. So he found a hotel elsewhere. Playa del Carmen was packed with tourists, and hotel rooms were hard to come by. Rozzi had to settle for a dump of an inn a few blocks away that had a power outage almost immediately after he checked in. Rozzi also had no water.

On Friday, February 27, the Interpol officers, using the FBI's pictures, identified Ghantt at the hotel, where the fugitive was sitting by the pool. They did not arrest him, knowing they needed to closely coordinate that action with the FBI. In addition, they needed to ask Rozzi to confirm the ID. Rozzi walked into the hotel and noticed the man in the lobby. It was Ghantt.

In Charlotte, the FBI remained uncertain about when to arrest everybody. The Interpol officers continued tracking Ghantt, waiting for Rozzi to give the signal. Meanwhile, Rozzi waited for orders from North Carolina, where agents were listening to Mike McKinney and Steve Chambers plot to assassinate Ghantt. But since McKinney's trip to Mexico was being delayed, there was no rush. The FBI would take its chances at finding the stolen money first.

The key to the whole equation, of course, was the Interpol officers' ability to keep track of Ghantt. To Rozzi's dismay, that was not a given.

Rozzi was stationed for hours at a time around the corner from the Hotel La Tortuga. There, he waited on the street to trail Ghantt's followers at a distance, in case they shadowed Ghantt out of the hotel. On Sunday, March 1, Rozzi saw the Interpol officers leaving the hotel with perplexed looks on their faces. They had lost him.

Rozzi's heart sank. Luckily, though, it turned out Ghantt was not running from them. He did not even know they were there. He came back to the hotel a few hours later. After he was back in sight, Rozzi called the FBI in North Carolina and told Shaffer that they needed to act fast because the Interpol officers obviously were not well trained in surveillance. If they didn't arrest Ghantt soon, they risked losing him. "I can't promise you he's not going to get lost again, for good," Rozzi said.

Shaffer asked if they could wait a few hours. He also wanted Rozzi to see if his hosts could keep Ghantt overnight in Mexico after his arrest and not publicize anything until the next day. The FBI planned to arrest Ghantt's cohorts the next morning, Monday, March 2, because that was the day McKinney and Tommy Grant were to fly to Mexico. If the news got out too early that Ghantt had been arrested, the North Carolina suspects could get desperate. The FBI began lining up its own people and some local police officers so they could arrest all the suspects in North Carolina simultaneously.

Three hours later, as the sun was about to set, about five undercover Interpol officers approached David Scott Ghantt on a street near the Hotel La Tortuga. He was holding a laundry bag and apparently looking for a place to do a Sunday wash. Even before Ghantt noticed them, he seemed nervous, like he was scanning the streets for his killer.

One of the officers tapped him on the back and said, "Excuse me, sir."

Ghantt kept walking.

"Excuse me, sir," the officer said. "Could we see your passport?"

Ghantt froze. As the officers surrounded him, he showed a picture identification with the name Michael McKinney.

The Interpol officer who tapped him said, "You're not Mr. McKinney, are you, Mr. Ghantt?"

"No, I'm not," Ghantt said, turning his head and making eye contact for the first time with Rozzi, who was standing about five feet behind him. Ghantt seemed relieved to see an American among the crew. "Please," Ghantt said, staring at Rozzi, "tell me you're an FBI agent."

"Yes, I am," Rozzi said.

"I'm glad to see you," Ghantt said.

"I'm glad to see *you*, David," Rozzi said.

"You know, they wanted to kill me."

"I know," Rozzi said. "Don't talk about that now. We'll have a chance to talk."

The Shit Comes Down

WITH A HANDGUN UNDER HIS PILLOW, Steve Chambers was in a criminally rich man's slumber next to Michele when, just after six o'clock on Monday morning, March 2, there was a loud knock at the door.

Minutes earlier, outside his fancy house, about two dozen FBI agents and local police officers had adjusted their Kevlar bulletproof vests, rechecked their Sig Sauer, Glock, and Smith & Wesson handguns, and stealthily positioned themselves around his yard, away from the windows. Minutes before that, the agents had driven a caravan of SUVs and cars up the winding road that led to 503 Stuart Ridge, passing through a neighborhood of fancy homes that the agents themselves could not afford. John Wydra, Rick Shaffer, and the other agents parked their cars a few homes away from that of Steve Chambers and silently got ready, guns drawn.

Hearing the knocking, Steve rose from bed, rubbed his eyes, threw on a pair of boxers, and stumbled to the door. "Who is it?" he asked.

A man outside said he was a Gaston County police officer and that somebody had broken into Steve's furniture store. The police needed to talk to him.

Steve opened his door.

"FBI! Get down! Get down!" the agents yelled.

Steve dropped to the floor by the door, his world collapsing. "What the hell's going on?" he blurted. The agents quickly surrounded him, handcuffed him, and put him under arrest. He asked to speak to Phil King.

"Be careful," Shaffer advised the other agents preparing to occupy the home room by room. "There are kids in the house."

Pointing their guns and flashlights, Wydra and Gerry Kidd, a Charlotte-Mecklenburg sheriff's deputy, rushed the bedroom, where Michele Chambers was huddled under the covers. "Hands up!" Wydra and Kidd yelled together.

Michele obeyed, revealing that she was wearing nothing but her $43,000 diamond ring. Wydra still had his gun pointed at her. Michele, her hands in the air, realized her breasts were showing and moved to pull the covers around her.

"Hands back up!" Kidd shouted, worried she had a weapon in the bed.

Michele stood up, grabbed a bathrobe, and held it in front of her.

Wydra and the other agents were suspicious the robe contained a weapon. "Hands back up!" Wydra yelled.

For law-enforcement officers, a robe is a standard security check in a bedroom arrest. Wydra and the other male agents in the room turned away from Michele while a female agent checked the robe for weapons. It was clean. Michele put it on. Then she removed her diamond ring at the agents' direction, placing it on the bathroom vanity. She would be allowed to dress and pack a bag for her children, she was told. The agents quickly discovered a handgun under a pillow on the bed.

While other agents began to take inventory of the couple's assets, Michele found the perfect moment when absolutely nobody's eyes but her own were on the diamond ring. She palmed it; after all, it was hers, she figured. When she walked into another room to pack a bag for her children, who would have to stay with her parents while she was in custody, it hit her that she was going to jail. She put the ring inside her children's suitcase. She also packed her Rolex and a diamond tennis bracelet.

She then called her parents' house. Dennis Floyd answered. "I need you to come pick up the kids," she said.

Her stepfather did not understand why.

"Right now," Michele said. "Bye."

About the same time, five miles away in Gastonia, FBI agents poured into the Hampton Inn. From the front desk, one of them called room 403, inhabited by Michael McKinney. McKinney had fallen asleep only two and a half hours earlier. The book he was reading—*The Partner* by John Grisham, about a lawyer who fakes his own death and flees to Brazil with $90 million—was on his hotel night table. Groggy, he answered the telephone, figuring it was a wake-up call.

The voice on the phone asked if he was Mike McKinney.

He said he was.

The voice said the FBI was there and told him to open his door.

McKinney did, and agents swarmed into his room.

At the same time, about five miles away in Mount Holly, agents called the mobile home of Kelly Campbell, who was sleeping in her panties. The person on the phone told Kelly that it was the FBI, that she should open the door, and that she had better stay on the phone while doing so.

Kelly peeked through the window blinds. Police cars were everywhere. She grabbed a robe and opened the door. Agents rushed inside. A female agent made her drop the robe, checked it for weapons, and gave it back to her. An agent asked if she knew what this was about. "It's about the money stolen from Loomis Fargo," Kelly said. "That's the only thing the FBI has ever interviewed me about."

She put a shirt on and alerted the agents to her pistol on her nightstand. Annoyed by a female agent's glare, Kelly mouthed off: "What are you looking at?" The agent shrugged her off.

Fourteen agents were present. They began looking through the home.

At the same time, twelve miles away in Belmont, agents knocked on the door of Eric Payne's mobile home. Eric yawned and walked to the door in his boxers. He figured it was a relative, though he had no idea who or why, since it was so early. He opened the door to FBI agents, who swarmed inside.

Eric said he had done nothing wrong. Then the agents found $70,000 in cash in a closet.

He told them it was from gambling.

They responded that he must be pretty good at it.

Early on, it was shaping up to be the worst day of their lives.

Shortly after the arrest, Michele asked if she could smoke a cigarette, and agent Erik Blowers, armed with a seizure warrant, deadpanned back, "Not in *my* house!"

Steve and Michele had made the steepest ascent of the social ladder after the heist, and their fall back down had already begun. They were taken in separate FBI cars to the agency's Charlotte headquarters for interviews. When they hit Interstate 85, they were driving the exact same highway—and in the exact opposite direction—that the group had traveled with the stolen money the evening of the heist.

That October night, and afterward, Steve had sworn his cohorts to keep their mouths shut if they were ever arrested. Now, five months later, knowing he probably faced the longest sentence of those arrested, Steve decided right away to do what was best for Steve—namely, to tell the FBI about every single person involved. It's a paradox of multiple-defendant criminal investigations that the person who has done the most wrong has the most to tell prosecutors, and therefore has the most to gain by telling it as soon as possible. If Steve told the feds about everybody and promised to testify against them if they claimed innocence, he could expect leniency at sentencing. Those were the rules. People with less guilt generally have fewer such points to play. It isn't fair, but that's how the system functions.

Steve had this in mind when, at about eight that morning, he found himself in an interview room at the FBI's offices in downtown Charlotte with agents Ray Duda and Bob Drdak, and David Sousa of the IRS. The agents advised him of his Miranda rights, and Steve waived them, agreeing to be interviewed. Then he told them almost everything that popped into his mind. The agents listened intently and took notes.

It was Kelly Campbell, Steve said, who approached him with the heist idea, saying she knew someone who worked at Loomis who might help out. He talked about getting Eric Payne and Scott Grant to assist, and of getting Mike McKinney to try and murder David Ghantt in Mexico. The most recent plan, he said, was for McKinney and Steve's cousin Nathan to fly to Mexico that very morning. Nathan knew nothing about the murder plot but would give Ghantt money while McKinney watched the delivery. McKinney would then trail Ghantt afterward.

Steve also told the feds about buying the BMW, Kelly's minivan, and Michele's $43,000 diamond ring. He talked about getting the $200,000 cashier's check at First Union with the help of Mike and Kim Goodman. He mentioned his furniture store purchase and the possible nightclub deal. He talked about how he had paid Nathan Grant to keep the stolen money in storage facilities, until around $2 million was stolen around Thanksgiving. The feds did not know whether to believe him on this one, wondering if he had really hidden that money somewhere in case he was arrested.

Steve named all the people he had paid to store money in safe-deposit boxes: Michele's parents, his own parents, Calvin Hodge, and David Craig, among others. He said he never revealed the source of the money to any of these people, but rather told them it came from bookmaking or gambling. The same information gap was true concerning his lawyer, Jeff Guller, who, he told the FBI, had managed his house purchase and received $10,000 to hold more than $400,000 of Steve's cash at his law office. Guller was also helping with other yet-to-be-completed transactions, Steve told the feds.

In a separate room, Michele sat with agents John Wydra and Lucie VonderHaar. "I don't have anything to say," Michele said. "I'm not talking."

On a dry-erase board near her was an FBI chronology, in blue magic marker, of her and Steve's activities after the heist. She stuck to her guns.

Wydra played bad cop. After Michele's continued refusals to talk, Wydra stormed out of the interview room, quickly returned with a folder, and slammed it down on the table in front of her. "You know what this is? These are pictures of you, Michele. I know you're involved in this."

Michele still would not talk.

Wydra stormed out of the room again. He quickly returned, this time with a videotape. "We got you on videotape," he said. "Making bank deposits."

Michele resisted for several hours. Nothing worked on her.

"Michele, we know everything," Wydra said. "They're all in there. They're all talking. And they're all pointing the finger at you."

Michele still would not tell the truth.

After conferring, the agents decided to have Steve talk to her. They brought him in and left them alone. Steve was crying, the sight of which terrified Michele. "I'm working it out," he told her. "Just tell them what you know."

Michele figured she could not count on Steve to protect her anymore. When he left, she started spilling the beans, telling the agents about the house purchase and the furniture store. She even revealed that she remembered counting more than $14 million at their home the night of the crime. She also talked about the safe-deposit boxes.

They talked about her breasts. She said she had gotten the implants in December 1996, before the heist occurred. During the investigation, the FBI had thought she used heist money for them and had written so in affidavits that were filed in the courthouse and were about to be released to the media.

She told the agents she had not known, at first, that the money came from Loomis Fargo.

Wydra said she was lying.

She said she thought Steve got it in return for holding money for "some friends up north." After the media coverage of the heist, though, she started to wonder. But she preferred not to know for certain, so she never asked, she said.

In a different room, FBI agents Rick Schwein and Thomas Widman were interrogating Kelly Campbell. She, too, was obstinate at first, until they showed her a surveillance picture of herself talking on the phone at Nichols Food Store.

"Well, this is what happened," Kelly said. She told them about the plan, saying Steve Chambers, not she, was the driving force. She said she had fed information about David Ghantt's location in Mexico to Steve, and that there was a murder plot that Chambers and his supposed hit man obviously could not pull off. "Them S.O.B.s have been going down since October and could not get close enough to kill him. *I* could've gone down there, and done it myself," she said to the agents.

She said she knew Ghantt had a crush on her and that she used his feelings to spur him to commit the theft, even paging him with 143 the day of the heist to encourage him. "How many chances do you get to talk someone into stealing $17 million for you?" she asked.

In another room, Wydra and Dick Womble were meeting resistance from Eric Payne, who denied any involvement.

"Steve Chambers is ratting you out," Womble said. "Kelly's in another room, and she's ratting you out."

Still, Eric resisted. He acknowledged knowing Steve but would not admit to helping in the Loomis Fargo theft. He also said nothing about his wife's and sisters' breast implants.

"Just send him to jail," Wydra said to Womble.

"I'm already going to jail," Payne shot back, knowing what was coming.

The Loomis thieves were not the only people in trouble.

A warrant allowed the FBI to seize assets from the business trust account of attorney Jeff Guller. Agents Bart Boodee and Charlie Daly drove to Guller's office on Main Street in Gastonia the morning of the arrests. They walked inside and up the steps to the reception area. Guller was in his back office. He came out. The agents identified themselves and presented the seizure warrant. Guller invited them into his office.

They asked if he had done business with anybody listed on the warrant.

He said yes, that he had done two real-estate deals with Steve Chambers—one for a $635,000 house and one for a $62,000 home in Lincoln County, and that the $635,000 house closing had involved cashier's checks. When asked, he said he did not know the source of Steve's money for the closings. He said that he had represented Chambers on worthless-check charges, that he had helped Chambers with papers for his furniture store, and that he had done some legal work for Kelly Campbell, whose name also was on the warrant.

The agents let him know that Chambers and Campbell had been

arrested for involvement in the Loomis Fargo heist.

Guller told them he was worried his business trust account was going to be frozen, because another client had a refinancing deal he needed to conduct the next day.

The agents told him he probably did not have to worry about that.

Soon after the arrests, the mayor of Cramerton called the *Charlotte Observer* to report unusual activity on Cramer Mountain. FBI agents were doing things probably related to the Loomis Fargo heist from last year, she told a reporter. Gary German called the newspaper, too. Photographers and TV camera crews were staked out at the scene by eight o'clock that morning.

The FBI held a packed press conference in Charlotte at eleven o'clock. Most of the questions were fielded by United States attorney Mark Calloway and William Perry of the FBI. They did not reveal many details, just some basics. They said that they had found Ghantt in Playa del Carmen; that he had been moving around Mexico since the heist; that he had significant help in North Carolina in planning and executing the crime; and that the FBI had charged at least two of his cohorts with trying to kill him. Perry said the FBI had recently obtained search warrants to look through the homes of various defendants in the Charlotte area, and that the reporters could obtain copies of a relevant affidavit at the federal courthouse.

For reporters, the forty-three-page affidavit was a gold mine of details about the defendants' extravagance. A quick glance made it obvious this story would be unforgettable. Breast implants? Liposuction? A $43,000 ring and a $635,000 house? The details topped the TV news. Almost everybody watching was amused except for Sandra Floyd, Michele's mother, who was in the waiting room of Carolinas Medical Center, where her mother had just gone for tests. She heard her daughter's name on the news and started crying. Sandra had really believed all that money was from gambling. The other people in the waiting room saw her crying and tried to comfort her, thinking somebody she knew had just died.

As for the defendants themselves, most were scheduled to make their first court appearance at two that afternoon.

The FBI had seven people in custody. Most of them were led into Charlotte's imposing federal courthouse in the Charles R. Jonas Federal Building for an appearance before Magistrate-Judge Carl Horn.

The courthouse and its tree-lined plaza were located four blocks from the NationsBank Building and within walking distance of Ericsson Stadium, home of the Carolina Panthers football team. The heist hearing took place in a small courtroom on the first floor with deep blue carpet and two and a half rows of benches that fit only twenty spectators. About ten more people could fit, standing, in the aisle. On this day, there were more reporters present than family members of the defendants.

The purpose of the initial hearing was to determine only whether the defendants, who were seated one at a time at a polished wooden table just a few feet from the prosecutor's table, could afford their own lawyers or would need court-appointed ones.

"You're not employed and have no assets," Horn said to Kelly Campbell while reviewing her paperwork. "You do have $5,000 in cash, is that right?"

Kelly, wearing blue-camouflage overalls, said the judge was correct but that her money had probably been confiscated.

She was right. The feds were scouring the defendants' homes, armed with search warrants. The FBI and federal marshals took everything they thought had been criminally accumulated.

The most bizarre scene occurred at the Chambers home, where marshals were removing furniture, paintings, a grand piano, and other luxuries before an amazed audience of neighbors, who had no idea they lived so close to the heist's beneficiaries. The neighbors watched a steady stream from the house over the course of the day—the velvet Elvis, a Confederate throw blanket, a large oil painting of dogs in military clothes, the piano, two bronze statues of nude men, a white porcelain statue of three nude women, a sculpture of a headless man, a ceramic white elephant, a brass pineapple, gold-framed oil paintings of zebras, Dallas Cowboys team plaques, naked-women bookends, a statue of a fat chef, a trumpet. Through a first-floor window of the house, an agent could be seen feeding stacks of money into a bill-counting machine. Other agents removed guns found in the home—a Mossberg twelve-gauge shotgun, a Beretta handgun, and an Interarms .38—along with fifty-four pieces of jewelry.

Two miles away at the furniture store, agents were removing the inventory. Mike Staley came by and explained that he was owed about $50,000 on the business. But he lacked a written contract and knew almost immediately that he would see none of that money. He was right.

In the courtroom, Steve told Judge Horn that all he now owned were eight acres and a double-wide trailer in Lincoln County, where his cousin Nathan Grant was living.

Without missing a beat, Horn turned to federal prosecutor David Keesler and asked, "Is there any intent to seize that property?"

Agents counted stacks of stolen cash inside the Chambers home on the day of the arrests.
Robert Lahser / CHARLOTTE OBSERVER

Keesler said it had already been done.

Horn looked back at Steve and said, "You just became eligible for a court-appointed lawyer. Congratulations."

The courtroom crowd was still too shocked by the goings-on to laugh at the irony of the rich man's need for a court-appointed attorney. The judge kept Kelly, Steve and Michele, Eric Payne, Mike McKinney, and Nathan Grant in jail, assigning all of them court-appointed lawyers. Their bond hearings were scheduled for March 5, three days away.

On their way back to jail, the defendants walked outside the courthouse into a transfer van. Kelly and Michele went separately from the male defendants. As the news cameras stationed near the van clicked away, Kelly decided to act goofy. She waved with her handcuffed hands and made a silly face, sticking out her tongue and cocking her eyes. Behind her, Michele grinned.

The eighth suspect arrested, Scott Grant, had peacefully turned himself in to FBI agents waiting at his home early in the afternoon, after hearing the news and figuring the feds were looking for him. He drove to his mobile home, got out of his car, and said, "Here I am."

An agent asked, "Who are you?"

"Scott Grant."

"You're the man we're looking for."

They let him change his clothes. Everybody who lived nearby watched as he left.

David Ghantt had a seat on US Airways flight 1514 from Cancun to Charlotte, which took off while his codefendants made their first court appearances. He ate a turkey sandwich. Mark Rozzi, who had paid Ghantt's bill at the Hotel La Tortuga on behalf of the FBI, sat next to him. As they soared above Florida in the early afternoon on March 2, David realized it was the first time he had been in the United States since the heist. He did not know exactly what awaited him when he landed, other than jail. He understood that his parents and other FBI agents would be very excited to see him.

It was rare for a fugitive to be so happy to see the authorities. The evening of his arrest on the streets of Playa del Carmen, the cops had taken him back to the Hotel La Tortuga. Two had spent the night to keep an eye on him. He was not surprised or miffed that they made him sleep handcuffed to the bed.

In the morning, as David was processed to leave the country, the Mexican authorities told him that because he had lived there with a fake ID—that of Mike McKinney—he could not travel back to Mexico for one year. David wondered whether they were kidding. It was unlikely he'd be traveling *anywhere* for a year.

Actually, the fake-ID charge helped the FBI, because it meant the agents did not have to worry about extradition hearings over the bank larceny. Foreigners living under fake IDs get kicked out.

When he boarded the plane, David Ghantt officially entered FBI custody. He and Rozzi got on first and headed to the back row.

Ghantt agreed to waive his Miranda rights, meaning Rozzi could interview him and get answers. But before Rozzi started, his curiosity got the best of him. "What was up with you and Kelly Campbell?" he asked.

Ghantt looked down, and Rozzi noticed his eyes moisten. "I was in love with her," he said.

Rozzi, still curious, asked how far things had gone.

"I only kissed her," Ghantt said. "I only kissed her one time. Pretty expensive fuckin' kiss, wasn't it?"

Then Rozzi began his formal interview. He asked questions in a whisper. Where had Ghantt stayed in Mexico? Whom had he talked to? How had he gotten involved in the first place? While writing Ghantt's answers in a notebook, Rozzi noticed that the flight attendants were watching them wide-eyed. Nearby passengers were suspending their own conversations to listen in and were quietly saying things to each other like "Holy shit! That's the guy!" News of the heist arrests had broken that morning. Some of the flight attendants on the plane had heard about it while in Charlotte earlier that day.

Ghantt told Rozzi how he had stolen the money, how he had worked with Kelly Campbell to make the heist happen, how he had grown suspicious his cohorts were working to kill him.

Rozzi said the FBI believed Kelly Campbell was involved in the murder plot. He had come to Mexico with tapes of recorded conversations, just in case David decided to resist talking to the feds. Rozzi offered to play some to convince David of her motives.

David was not in the mood. He looked at the floor. He realized without hearing the tapes that he had been duped more than he previously thought. David was anxious to tell Rozzi everything, anxious to make sure the FBI knew he was something of a victim here. After all, he had feared for his life only one day earlier.

And Rozzi was anxious to write down everything David said, to

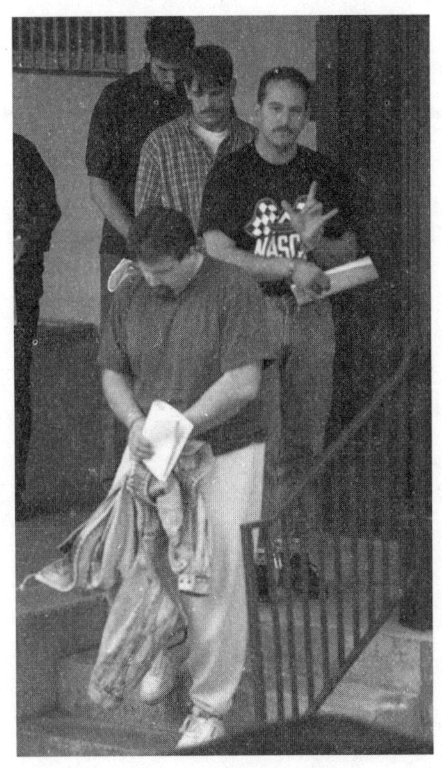

Steve Chambers is followed by Eric Payne, Nathan Grant, and Mike McKinney as they leave Charlotte's federal courthouse and head for jail shortly after their arrests.
Laura Mueller / CHARLOTTE OBSERVER

ask every possible question. He didn't know that back in North Carolina, the other defendants were falling over like bowling pins.

Rozzi told Ghantt that the FBI had contacted his relatives and that they might be waiting for his flight. When the plane landed at five that afternoon, Rozzi and Ghantt were the last to get off. The other passengers, reaching for their items in the overhead bins, could not help glancing again at David before leaving. When all the other passengers were off, the FBI's Rick Shaffer came to the plane door to escort David. Inside the plane, agent Ray Duda informed Rozzi that the other defendants were confessing to various roles.

David looked around but could not find his relatives. On the ground, before Ghantt entered an FBI car, Rozzi introduced agent Duda to him. "Nice to meet you, David," Duda said. "I gotta ask you one thing. What was going on between you and Kelly Campbell?"

Rozzi blanched. He had not told Duda that he had asked the same question.

Ghantt looked stunned. This was the first question of *two* agents? He asked Rozzi, "Is he joking? Are you guys kidding me?"

Life could have been worse for David Ghantt. Despite stealing $17 million, he was charged only with bank larceny and money laundering. And though those crimes technically had a combined maximum sentence of thirty years, he likely would be imprisoned less than ten years if he pleaded guilty, because he lacked a prior record.

In jail, he found himself treated like a minor celebrity, even a hero. He had taken the money and run, his fellow inmates told him. That took guts.

David's mother came to see him that first night in jail. His family members had heard about his arrest only through the news. They had not learned his flight information in time to meet him at the airport.

He quickly saw that his mother still loved and supported him. Sue Ghantt did not yell at him for abandoning her. "You're my son," she said. "I love you." She told him how close she and Tammy had grown through the previous five months.

David said Tammy probably hated him.

Sue Ghantt advised him to call her.

He did so a little later. It was a tense conversation. She expected the call, having talked to his mother, but Tammy was still nervous.

David told her he was scared to talk to her but that he still cared about her. He still loved her, he said.

She still loved him, though at the moment she was not in a lovey-dovey mood. "I thought I'd never see you again," she said.

"I thought I'd never see *you* again either," he said.

Her first questions were simple. Why did he do this to her? If he still loved her, why didn't he call while he was away?

He said that he wanted to protect her, that he didn't want to get her involved, that he figured the FBI would consider her an accessory if they talked.

Tammy had heard in the news about his so-called relationship with Kelly Campbell.

She was just a friend, David said. Not much more.

Tammy asked, "Did you have sex with her?"

"No," David said. "And that's the truth."

That made Tammy feel a lot better. Still, after they hung up, she started to cry. It had been an emotional day.

It was a less emotional day for Jody and Jennifer Calloway. More than three months after taking money from Steve's storage facility, the Calloways remained in Colorado. They had recently augmented their vehicle collection with a used Corvette and a Ford Mustang. Their move stayed beneath the radar of the FBI and the defendants, most of whom did not know them. Jody was operating a small business called Rocky Mountain Woodworking with a man named Joseph Hamilton. Jody was the principal financier, giving his partner more than $50,000.

The M&M's Contest

On Tuesday, March 3, 1998, the day after the bulk of the arrests, the *Charlotte Observer*'s main headline read, simply, "Eight Jailed in Huge Heist." "Is This the Gang That Couldn't Think Straight?" read another front-page headline, over an article by columnist Tommy Tomlinson that read, in part, "There is no polite way to say this: These folks are not exactly the brightest bulbs in the chandelier," having engaged so soon after the theft in "five months of high rolling that would make Richie Rich blush."

The *Observer*'s front page also had a list, based on FBI documents, of the suspects' largest purchases: the $635,000 house, the BMW Z-3, the $43,000 diamond ring, a leased pickup truck, and Michele's breast implants, which the FBI wrongly believed she bought with heist proceeds. Steve and Michele's velvet Elvis was starting to become a joke around Charlotte.

In local newsrooms, reporters continued pulling up information on attorney Jeff Guller. He was not charged with anything, but his name was conspicuously included in that main FBI affidavit, and the feds were searching his law office on Gastonia's Main Street. It was unclear to the local media whether Guller's involvement in the heist aftermath was criminal. The FBI affidavit mentioned that he had handled Steve's house purchase and that there had been telephone contact between them, but it did not reveal any substantive details.

At Guller's request, agents Boodee and Daley returned to his office on March 3 to discuss keeping his trust fund unfrozen for his other client's deal. The agents had been briefed on what Steve Chambers told the FBI about keeping massive amounts of cash in Guller's office for several weeks. If that was true, Guller could be open to criminal charges. Indicting a lawyer for federal money laundering had never happened in that part of North Carolina.

The agents asked Guller if Steve ever brought him a large stash of money.

Yes, Guller told them, Steve had brought over a black suitcase full of cash before the house closing and unzipped it to show the cash inside. He discussed with Guller whether to use it for the closing. Guller told Steve that using the cash meant he would have to sign a form indicating its source. Steve did not want to do that, so they agreed that instead he would secure cashier's checks for the required amount. Steve then took the suitcase and left his office, Guller said.

Boodee pressed him. "Mr. Guller, was there any time when the suitcase or any other large amount of money was left with you in your office?"

Guller said, "There might've been a time during that conversation when Chambers got up and left and went out to his car for ten minutes or so, and while he was out at his car, the suitcase was with me alone here in the office." But Steve soon returned to the office, retrieved the suitcase, and left, Guller said.

Boodee pressed him again. "Are you certain there was not a time in your dealings with Mr. Chambers that Mr. Chambers left money in your office?"

"No," Guller said. "Absolutely not. Never, ever, on any occasion would I have done that."

"This is an important issue we're talking about," Boodee said. "It's serious. It's a felony to lie or intentionally provide false or fictitious information to an FBI agent. . . . We can reexamine what you've said if you want to revisit it with me."

Guller sat quietly, then said, "Remember when I told you about Mr. Chambers leaving the money? It didn't happen that way." He told Boodee how Steve had brought the suitcase to the office. This time, he mentioned that he, Guller, had never looked inside it.

"What if it was drugs inside the suitcase?" Boodee asked.

"I don't know, but I would've told him to go to hell. I presumed it was currency, and I should have told him to go to hell anyway."

They talked again about the October discussions between Guller and Steve involving the house purchase. Guller admitted that Steve had indeed left the bag of cash for about two weeks, before Guller returned it after taking out $10,000 for himself. He said Steve insisted he take the money, first saying it was payment for storing the bag and then, after Guller repeatedly declined, calling it a Christmas gift. Guller also told the agents about two discussed deals that never happened—the land for Kelly Campbell's husband and the nightclub for Steve. He said Steve had asked if it was possible to buy the land for Kelly's husband under a phony name, and that he replied it was not.

Boodee had a tape recorder and cassettes with wiretapped conversations. When Guller said that, Boodee fast-forwarded to a point in a conversation between Guller and Steve when Guller said it was indeed possible to put property in a fictitious name. The tape made it clear that the FBI was considering charging Guller as a heist accomplice.

Guller admitted to Boodee that the tape made him sound bad. "I was bullshitting my client to make him feel good." He said he eventually would have told Steve it was illegal. He admitted he had probably exercised bad judgment. "I should not have told him I was going to do it under an assumed name."

Boodee then asked about the conversation—recorded, of course—in which Guller and Steve discussed paying up to $250,000 to get a pardon for Steve's felony convictions.

Again, Guller said he was just bullshitting, and that he never intended to participate in a bribe.

The federal courthouse was already closed when David Ghantt's plane landed after five o'clock the day everyone else was arrested, so his first court appearance was Tuesday, March 3. Wearing an orange jail uniform, he walked into Carl Horn's courtroom. His family was there—Tammy, his parents, his sisters. David stared at them on his

After her arrest, Michele Chambers (*center*) told the FBI about the house purchase. She also told them she helped count more than $14 million the night of the crime.
Laura Mueller / CHARLOTTE OBSERVER

way to the defendant's table. His eyes brushed over Tammy. It was the first time he had seen her face in five months. She was in the first row, and she seemed glad he was alive, but as he expected, she also looked stunned and hurt.

David told Judge Horn that he had no cash. Horn assigned him a court-appointed lawyer.

As David walked out of the courtroom after this brief appearance, he stared a few seconds at his family and whispered, to his mother and sister, "I love you." Then he stared at Tammy. She stared back. Neither said anything. Only days earlier, each had figured on never seeing the other one again.

The other defendants, awaiting Thursday's bond hearing, were the subjects of newly public FBI affidavits filed earlier in the day at the federal courthouse. Those affidavits revealed that at least three of them—Kelly Campbell, Steve Chambers, and Eric Payne—had admitted involvement in the heist.

From Playa del Carmen, *Observer* reporter Joe DePriest wrote a story about Ghantt that would provide weeks of laughter back home. "He was a peculiar *norteamericano* in a Caribbean town known for its oddballs," the story began, before quoting a Hotel La Tortuga receptionist who said Ghantt spent most of his time there alone in his room eating M&M's, listening to the Eagles, smoking Marlboro Lights, and reading comic books. If he went out, she said, Ghantt liked eating at Burger King and drinking tequila at a nearby bar, Capitan Tutex. Sometimes, he sat by the hotel pool, which was next to his room.

On Wednesday, the radio and TV stations devoured these details, especially the part about the M&M's. The story confirmed the stereotype—always good for laughs on Southern radio—about the simple tastes of working-class guys. In this case, the guy stole $17 million and still wanted nothing more out of life than cigarettes, candy, cheap liquor, and the Eagles. An FM radio station, WLNK, announced a call-in contest for a week-long trip to Playa del Carmen. The winner would stay at the Hotel La Tortuga and receive the following: $1,000 in cash with a phony bank wrapping around it, a supply of M&M's, Eagles CDs, comic books, and a Wonderbra, in honor of the heist-financed breast implants.

Other media had fun, too. On the *John Boy & Billy Big Show*, a recurring character named Marvin Webster drew laughs. "The dude that actually stole the money," Webster said on the radio, "he's down in some crappy hotel room with a big stack of comic books, a copy of *Hotel California*, and he's living off M&M's in the mini-bar, layin' low, waiting for the high sign. Meanwhile, his friends back home are running around like the Home Shopping Club on crack! Did you see some of the stuff they bought? Chevy Tahoe, BMW Z-3, bunch of motorcycles. Yeah, no way this could've attracted any attention. They bought two or three computers. Ten-thousand-dollar pool table. Forty-thousand-dollar diamond ring. One guy bought his wife some new boobs. . . . These dudes pull the crime of the century [and] would've gotten away with it except they couldn't walk into the 7-Eleven without buying $1,500 worth of beef jerky!"

The hilarity took a hiatus on Thursday, March 5, when the families came to court to plead with Judge Horn to free the defendants until their trials. More than a hundred relatives and friends attended, so the judge operated out of a bigger courtroom.

All the defendants had well-respected court-appointed lawyers. The first one to argue before Judge Horn was Noell Tin, the attorney for David Ghantt. Tin's goal, and that of all the attorneys, was to persuade the judge that his client would not flee or do anything illegal while free before trial—that his client had reasons to stick around that outweighed the incentive to leave. Tin tried to drum up sympathy for Ghantt by noting that he had been the subject of a murder plot. He told the judge that Ghantt had strong community ties that ensured he would stay in North Carolina and go to court on schedule. "I have a client who not surprisingly has a very substantial turnout for his family, to demonstrate his family ties," said Tin. He turned around to Ghantt's relatives and asked, "Can y'all stand up?"

More than a dozen people rose. One of them, David's mother, walked across the courtroom's light blue carpet to the witness stand to testify before the judge. "I just want you to know," Sue Ghantt told Horn, "we have a very fine son. He's always been honest and trustworthy and dependable [and] loving and kind. He has not ever been violent."

Her testimony was jaw-dropping. Trustworthy? Dependable? It seemed silly, even coming from someone's mother. The guy had stolen millions of dollars and run away! If it had worked out, he would never have been heard from again. At the same time, his mother was heartbreaking to watch. She was in her fifties and had curly, graying hair and glasses. She looked like a mother who loved her son unconditionally, because she knew that, deep down, he had a good heart and would not hurt a fly. He meant so much to her and his dad and his sisters.

"It appears he may have made a mistake," Sue Ghantt continued, "but we love him, and we support him, and we care for him. And I don't think you would regret letting him out in our care. We would appreciate it very much."

Tin, Ghantt's attorney, spoke next. He told the judge that, if freed on bond, Ghantt could live with a relative in Gastonia or with his parents in Hendersonville. It would not be terribly difficult for him to find a job, Tin said. "There is only one other thing I can say to Your Honor, which is that my client is presumed innocent. There is a temptation to presume we know exactly what happened at this point, [but] the statutory and constitutional law is simple: He is treated simply as a man who is presumed innocent. He's never been arrested in his life. And those kinds of people ordinarily get bond in federal court. And sometimes, someone goes out of the country for reasons other than flight from law enforcement."

Prosecutor David Keesler said that was hogwash. First of all, Keesler said, between $6.6 million and $8 million was still missing. Maybe Ghantt knew its location and would run away with it if freed. Ghantt already had abused a position of trust at Loomis Fargo, using his access to money to commit the crime, he reminded the judge. "I mention this because this is a case about greed, and it's a case about what some people will do for money. None of these defendants ought to be allowed out when that sort of money is still out there, and we don't know where it is." The weight of the evidence was overwhelming, Keesler said. "Mr. Ghantt is on videotape removing money from the Loomis facility. Seventeen-plus million dollars of money."

Judge Horn, to no one's surprise, decided to keep Ghantt locked up. The evidence against him was compelling, he said. He noted that Ghantt would have a better chance at bail if the missing money was found.

Next up was Scott Grant. Another federal prosecutor, Brian Whisler, told the judge that other defendants placed Grant at the heist scene. He said that Grant helped off-load the money from the Loomis van with Eric Payne and Steve Chambers, who had planned to hire Grant at his furniture store. "He was there at the beginning," Whisler said. "He's been intimately involved."

Grant's stepmother, Lillie Finley, told Horn that both Scott and his accused brother, Nathan, could live with her if the judge freed them.

Grant's father, Bob Finley, testified that Scott had only $90 in his bank account, far too little to allow him to skip town.

The judge was not sympathetic. Grant would stay in jail.

Next, it was Kelly Campbell's turn. Horn started by saying the evidence showed that Kelly helped mastermind the heist, that she used a lot of marijuana, and that she knew of the murder plot against Ghantt.

David Ghantt, sitting next to Campbell in the courtroom, stared at her with hurt in his eyes when he heard this, shaking his head.

Keesler stood up. "She was the link," he said, "between David Scott Ghantt, who was then employed at Loomis, and Mr. Chambers and the rest of these folks." She helped Ghantt get his phony ID to leave the country, and she had admitted her role to the FBI, Keesler said.

When Kelly's lawyer, James Gronquist, asked her family to stand, three rows of people—her pastor; her parents; her husband, Jimmy; and her two children—complied.

Her mother, Colleen Elmore, testified on her behalf, saying Kelly, if freed, could live with her and work for her brother's construction business until her trial. "I know this is bad, and my daughter has to pay for what she's done, but I'm just asking you to let her go home until she goes to trial and be with her kids, because they may not see her until they're half-grown. I promise you I will handcuff her to my wrist if I have to, to see that she don't go nowhere. It's not right for them li'l young'uns not to get to be with their mama."

Judge Horn kept Kelly in jail, though he seemed sympathetic. "This is a very sad situation," he said, "when you have children and families hurt by very poor choices that other family members make. I have never seen a defendant who, once they've been caught, doesn't wish that they had made a different choice earlier."

Mike McKinney stood next before the judge. He knew what was going to happen.

Judge Horn reviewed his paperwork and noted his prior convictions for cocaine possession and driving while impaired.

Whisler noted that McKinney was the one being paid to murder Ghantt.

Horn kept him in jail.

Next, the judge reviewed Eric Payne's paperwork.

The prosecutors noted he was part of the heist itself and was later caught on a wiretap talking about trying to intimidate Steve's old friend from Belmont Hosiery, who Payne thought was spreading rumors about the defendants' involvement in the heist.

Payne's lawyer, Chris Connelly, said his client was not a risk to flee and should be released from jail until his trial. "If he wanted to flee, he could have fled a long time ago and possibly not been apprehended," Connelly said. "But he stayed right here where he was, worked the same job, lived with his family, tried to get a better job, tried to pay off his trailer, tried to buy the land underneath it."

Judge Horn kept him in jail.

The next-to-last defendant up for bond was Michele Chambers. Whisler called her one of the prime beneficiaries of the heist. He mentioned how she had walked into a bank with a briefcase of money and asked how much she could deposit without the filing of paperwork.

Her lawyer, Andy Culler, acknowledged her spending habits of the last five months but argued to Judge Horn that, in the scheme of things, Michele was just "a young woman who is doing what she is told, rather than necessarily planning and directing activities."

Michele's mother took the stand. Sandra Floyd told the judge that Michele had struggled before she met Steve Chambers because her first husband did not pay enough to support their children. She said Michele could stay at her house if freed.

Keesler was geared to pounce. He asked Sandra Floyd if she was surprised that Michele and Steve could buy their furniture store and their big house a few months back.

"I was never really told exactly where or how they made their money," Sandra Floyd said. She added that Michele told her it came from gambling.

Judge Horn asked her, "Did your daughter show you her $43,000 ring?"

"I saw several rings she wore," Floyd said.

"Did they look like they were worth $100,000 to you?"

"Yes."

"Did you think that that came from gambling earnings? Financing?"

"I know that they were a gift from her husband for Christmas."

Horn kept Michele in jail.

Nathan Grant was the last defendant up for bond consideration.

His lawyer, Bob Michel, might as well have just sat and twiddled his thumbs.

Keesler told the judge that Nathan was scheduled to fly to Mexico with McKinney, and that he had received more than $70,000 from Steve Chambers.

Judge Horn kept him in jail.

As they left the courtroom in shackles, heading back to jail, David Ghantt and Kelly Campbell found themselves standing next to each other in a courthouse tunnel. David just looked at her.

"I'm sorry," Kelly said. "It wasn't me. It was Steve."

"Yeah, right," David said. He turned away, not making eye contact as they walked toward the van that returned them to their cells.

Later, Steve approached David and blamed Kelly for the murder plot. "When she got that money, she just went nuts," he said.

David said nothing. He looked away and watched several non-heist inmates, who were staring at them with amazement.

At that point, David was talking to Tammy every night. He felt he had someone there for him. Tammy felt like a wife again. The mood of their phone calls was slowly softening. Tammy still wanted to make their relationship work.

Inmates were not allowed to accept incoming calls, so David phoned her collect at night, making her laugh by identifying himself to the operator as "M&M's"—he had heard about the radio contest—or Rascals, their cat. They usually talked for about fifteen minutes.

Tammy sent him a picture of her. She beamed when he said he put it on the mirror in his cell to "pretty up the place."

She could tell he was enjoying his newfound celebrity. They talked about the episode of *America's Most Wanted* in which she pleaded for him to come home. He asked if her family taped it. He wanted to see it someday.

He said he had really missed her on Valentine's Day, while he was alone in Mexico. He told her that he didn't deserve her, that he knew the uncertainty had traumatized her.

She was still angry at him. The only way she could make sense of it was wondering if it was all meant to be, to give them another chance to improve on what apparently bothered him before the heist. She still treasured her pre-heist memories of him. She still had the key to their mobile home, which had been foreclosed on three months earlier, when she could not make the payments.

They talked about what they would do when he left prison—probably sometime around 2006 or 2007, he figured. They would move away from North Carolina, to a place where people would not know the name David Ghantt. Maybe she would open a tanning salon. He would open a tree-trimming service, or maybe a towing company.

Of Brain Size and Bust Size

JUST BECAUSE EIGHT PEOPLE WERE JAILED did not mean the FBI's investigation was over. The entire week after the arrests, federal agents drove around Gaston and Lincoln Counties, to banks and storage facilities and the homes of defendants, looking for portions of the stolen cash and the various vehicles, jewelry, and electronics bought with it. They searched in safe-deposit boxes and living rooms and bedrooms and kitchens.

Hours after they arrested Steve and Michele Chambers on March 2, agents found $565,602 in a cardboard box in the lower drawers of an office desk in their house. In the same room, in a plastic bag, they found keys for safe-deposit boxes.

The day after the arrests, FBI agent Ray Duda recovered $897,000 in cash from one safe-deposit box and $470,000 from another. Two days later, Duda and John Wydra discovered $360,000 in a box cosigned for by Steve Chambers and David Craig and $454,000 in a box cosigned for by Calvin Hodge and Michele Chambers. The day after that, they opened one containing $400,000. Nathan Grant and Amy Grigg had cosigned for it. Six-figure sums were also stashed in several other safe-deposit boxes, the signatories being Steve, his aliases, or other friends and relatives.

Also that week, at the Pack 'N' Stack Mini Storage in Cherryville, agents found, in a facility rented by Steve Chambers and Calvin Hodge, a blue barrel containing dry dog food on a piece of cloth. Under the cloth was $770,000 in cash.

By the time of Steve's bond hearing the following Tuesday, March 10, the FBI could account for almost $12.9 million of the stolen money, including the $3.3 million found in the Loomis van on October 6, 1997, two days after the heist. Brian Whisler, the assistant United States attorney at Steve's bond hearing, told Judge Horn that about $4.15 million remained missing, and that Steve should not be released until it was found.

Chris Fialko, the court-appointed lawyer for Steve, did not bother to argue his client's case. In fact, he had tried to cancel the bond hearing. He knew, from the results of the previous week's hearings, that the odds of Horn's freeing Steve Chambers were almost nil.

He was right. Steve was led back to jail.

The federal government was doing more than recovering stolen money. It was investigating the people who cosigned for the safe-deposit boxes. On Thursday, March 12, a grand jury returned a forty-nine-count indictment setting formal charges not only against the eight current defendants but also against nine other people, all of them relatives or friends of the first eight.

The new set of defendants included Michele's parents, Steve's parents, Steve's best man, Nathan Grant's fiancée, Eric Payne's wife, Calvin Hodge, and Calvin Hodge's father. They were all charged with money laundering for helping to hide the money. Each was freed on bond but was terrified by the prospect of the potential sentence. The twenty-year maximum penalty for money laundering seemed to guarantee at least some time locked up.

Among themselves, the prosecutors debated whether money-laundering charges were appropriate. Traditionally, money-laundering crimes involve schemes to turn stolen "dirty" money into "clean" money by running it through a seemingly legitimate business. But federal courts allow prosecutors to file a money-laundering charge when a specific act—obtaining safe-deposit boxes to hide dirty money—was performed with money that the defendant knew, or should have known, was illegally obtained. The crimes in question could seem more like concealment of stolen property than money laundering. But the harsher penalty for money laundering let prosecutors pressure defendants to plead guilty, which would qualify them for much lighter sentences than if their cases reached trial and they lost.

None of these "money-stuffers"—as the feds called the defendants who hid cash for Steve in safe-deposit boxes—were involved in the heist itself. Steve apparently did not tell any of them that the money came from the Loomis Fargo heist. Sandra and Dennis Floyd, for example, thought they were stowing Steve's gambling winnings. Sandra Floyd could not believe it was leading to criminal charges. The couple had received $40,000 from Steve and Michele and used $13,000 of it for a pickup truck and $3,000 for a 1.04-carat diamond ring.

Other defendants—David and Kelly, for example—were charged with money laundering, on top of the bank larceny charges, for essentially nothing more than spending their stolen money. Some defense attorneys complained that the spending was merely incidental to the bank larceny crime and was not worthy of separate money-laundering counts, which exposed the defendants to longer sentences. For example, David Ghantt faced up to ten years for the bank larceny but up to twenty for his money-laundering count, which charged him only with spending the money he stole.

The nine new defendants may have been shocked by their arrests, but at least they were free until their next court hearings. Meanwhile, all original eight defendants remained behind bars through March 20, when Nathan Grant formally pleaded guilty and was released on bond until his sentencing hearing. Nathan entered a guilty plea to one count of money laundering, implicating himself in storing $400,000 of stolen money in a safe-deposit box. The feds had more on him—for example, Steve Chambers paid him $70,000 to stash money just after the heist—but they agreed not to press other charges as part of the deal. His fiancée, Amy Grigg—charged the prior week with money laundering—sat in the first row of the courtroom watching the father of her child virtually ensure himself a prison sentence.

Nathan, a twenty-one-year-old mill worker, would not know his fate right away. In federal court, sentences are usually imposed a few months after conviction. The judge freed him on bond, determining him a safe bet to return to court for sentencing and, of course, to not swipe any of the missing money. He did not return to the mobile home where Steve had let him live after the heist; federal marshals had seized that. Nathan moved in with his mother.

Days later, his brother Scott pleaded guilty to bank larceny and money laundering. Scott Grant also agreed to testify against the other defendants, if needed. In return, prosecutors dropped a charge of accessory after the fact. The judge agreed to let him live with his mother until his sentencing hearing, setting the condition that he not talk to Nathan about the crime.

Scott's level of involvement was determined to be more severe than his brother's. Unlike Nathan, he had been part of the theft. Nathan, on the other hand, had received more stolen money. Steve Chambers told agents he promised Scott $200,000, but Scott had received only about $26,000, in increments of $6,000 or $7,000.

"He's remorseful about what transpired," Scott's lawyer, Keith Stroud, told the assembled press after the court hearing. "He wants to make the best of a bad situation."

Nathan Grant and Amy Grigg, in the courtroom for Scott's hearing, held hands as they watched him plead guilty. Oddly, the federal courtroom was developing a family atmosphere during the weeks of hearings, thanks to all the connections among the Chamberses, Floyds, Grants, and Paynes. Whoever was free on bond, it seemed, would come to watch their codefendants' hearings.

On Monday, March 30, Kelly Campbell, Michele Chambers, and Eric Payne were led into court in orange jail uniforms for another bond hearing, having appealed Judge Horn's decisions the week of the arrests. The presiding judge was Graham Mullen.

Prosecutor David Keesler wanted the trio to remain imprisoned. He acknowledged to Mullen that more of the missing money had been found—now, all but $2.6 million was accounted for—but he maintained that the three might know where that money was, and that they might flee with it. He described their involvement in the crime, noting that Kelly, for example, had helped plan the heist and had participated in the murder plot. He also recounted how the feds found $6,000 in cash in her mobile home.

Keesler told the judge how Michele helped rent the van used to move the stolen money and later spent some of the cash for her breast implants.

Michele's lawyer, Andy Culler, objected. He set the record straight by noting that Michele had the implants before the heist.

Judge Mullen ruled the three of them could leave jail, placing them under house arrest except for work and church. They would have to wear electronic ankle bracelets that would automatically alert the authorities if they left their homes without permission. Their relatives wept with joy after Mullen's ruling, which meant the defendants could spend time at home with their children before their expected prison sentences.

The judge warned Kelly, Michele, and Eric that if they fled, they would be caught. "You will be back here in your orange suits," he said.

The electronic monitoring equipment had to be connected to the defendants' home telephones. Setting it up took a few days. They stayed in jail until the systems were ready.

Charlotte Observer reporter Chip Wilson trekked to the home of Michele's parents after she was released from jail. He interviewed Michele on April 7. "I do want to go on record to say I didn't get breast implants with this money," she said, telling the people of the Carolinas that she paid for her new breasts in December 1996, ten months before the heist, and that she considered them a luxury. "It was something that I wanted to get. It increased my bust size, but it didn't decrease my brain size."

She complained that the FBI seized items she and Steve had owned before the heist, including an "I Love Mommy" ring. "A lot of it came from Wal-Mart," she said.

David Ghantt's lawyer thought that if Kelly Campbell was allowed

The stylishly dressed Michele Chambers heads to a court hearing seven weeks after her arrest. *Robert Lahser* / CHARLOTTE OBSERVER

out of jail on bond, David should be freed on bond as well. After all, Campbell had plotted to kill Ghantt, a more violent charge than anything Ghantt faced. If she was free, why shouldn't he be?

But on April 22, 1998, Judge Mullen decided—reluctantly, he said—to keep Ghantt and Steve Chambers locked up. "I can't get around the notion that this is a fellow that stayed gone for five months," Mullen said. He added that if he was keeping Ghantt locked up, he would certainly do the same to Chambers, who, facing the most serious charges of anyone in the case, "clearly has the strongest motive of any of these defendants to flee."

The government continued searching for the missing $2.6 million. Chambers continued to maintain it was stolen from him, after he himself had stolen it. "I'm not sure the government believes that," David Keesler said.

Heist trials were scheduled for October 1998, but most observers thought that few, if any, would be necessary. None of the defendants was seriously protesting the FBI's investigative methods, so it was looking like guilty pleas all around. There was strong evidence against almost everyone arrested. Even if the FBI could not prove that the people who helped Steve Chambers hide money knew he was involved in the heist, it could likely show they should have known he was up to something dirty. Why else would he offer to pay them to help store money or to get him checks, things he should have been able to do himself if the money were clean?

On April 24, Calvin Hodge pleaded guilty to money laundering, becoming the third defendant in the case to enter a guilty plea.

Meanwhile, FBI investigators pieced together a chronology of the five months after the heist. It was becoming clear that they had a strong case against Jeffrey Guller and some other people whose names were mentioned in the main affidavit released to the public after the arrests.

It was the talk of the town in Gastonia's legal community, which wondered what would happen to one of its own, a person many had known for decades. His friends hoped it was just a false rumor. Some speculated he would skip town.

Guller knew deep down that he might be in trouble, but he also knew that too much cooperation with the FBI could facilitate federal charges against him, and that he could lose his license to practice law.

His steadfast denials of wrongdoing only made the feds more determined. On June 2, 1998, a new indictment, charging Jeffrey Guller with money laundering, was made public. The most damning charge stated that he accepted a "bagful of currency" at his law office from Steve Chambers, stored it there at Steve's request, and took $10,000 for himself as a fee before returning it to Steve at a Gastonia fish camp the previous December. The indictment also told how Guller helped Steve and Michele buy their $635,000 house, depositing more than $400,000 from them into his trust account and then transferring it for the huge down payment.

Reporters researching the criminal background of Steve Chambers learned that Guller had been his attorney in the past. They noted that Guller represented Steve on charges of writing tens of thousands of dollars in bad checks and that, at about the same time, he helped Steve upgrade to a mansion.

In court on the day of his arrest, Guller sat silently as his lawyer, Calvin Murphy, entered a not-guilty plea. Also in the courtroom were Kim and Michael Goodman, whose roles in helping Steve and Michele convert $200,000 into a cashier's check had led to money-laundering charges against them under this latest indictment. Michele Chambers sat next to the Goodmans. She found herself facing an additional charge of bank fraud unrelated to the Loomis Fargo theft. Prosecutors were accusing her of using a false ID to get money from a NationsBank branch in Hickory the previous June, four months before the heist. The charge, if true, would back the FBI's internal assertion that she was involved in crime before October 4, 1997.

Eric Payne said he had no idea what he was getting into when he decided to help Steve Chambers. "I'd like to say I'm sorry to the government and my family and my children that I've hurt through this," he said on June 9, 1998, when he became the fourth heist defendant to plead guilty at the federal courthouse. "I'd like to put this all behind me and go on with my life."

Like Payne, Michele Chambers had been free on bail since early April. She took a job waitressing at Chili's restaurant in Gastonia. Despite all the recent publicity, few people recognized her at work or around town, which suited her just fine. It also suited her that the FBI had not found the diamond ring, the Rolex, and the bracelet she had brazenly swiped just after she was arrested. She had since hocked the Rolex to pay bills.

On August 3, 1998, she and Steve met in court for the first time since the arrests, becoming the next two people in the case to plead guilty. They sat next to each other at the defendants' table, he wearing an orange jail uniform and she wearing a sleeveless magenta dress. They whispered to each other several times. They also swore to tell the truth on the same Bible.

Michele's case was heard first. She pleaded guilty to bank larceny and money laundering. In return, the government dropped a charge of accessory after the fact.

She could hardly speak through her tears. "The anxiety medicine is supposed to keep me from doing what I'm doing right now," she said. Her weeping prevented her from reading a statement she had prepared for the occasion. Her lawyer, Andy Culler, shared it with the court on her behalf: "First, I'd like to say that I know what happened was wrong and I accept responsibility for my actions, but I'd also like to say that all of the people that are involved need to admit that Steve and I didn't do this thing alone. I am hoping that through my cooperation with this court and its affiliates, I can help to make certain that the truth finally does come out." In her statement, Michele apologized to Loomis Fargo, its insurance company, her children, the other defendants' children, and the friends and family of the people involved. She thanked God and her family for supporting her and professed her love for Steve: "I want to just tell you I love you and I'll be here for you. Thank you for loving me through all of the bad times in my life. You've always been here for me and helped me to be strong, and I know that one day God will bring us back together."

Steve, who looked like he had lost fifty pounds since his arrest, largely because of jailhouse food, was less verbal, answering the federal magistrate-judge's questions in a quiet voice. He pleaded guilty to charges of bank larceny, accessory to bank larceny, conspiracy to murder-for-hire, and thirteen counts of money laundering. In return, the government dropped three counts of possession of a firearm by a felon.

Outside the courthouse, Chris Fialko, Steve's attorney, told reporters that the remaining defendants in the case "need to understand that if they choose to go to trial, Steve will testify against them."

By the end of the week, six more defendants followed suit. Robert Chambers, Mary Chambers, Amy Payne, Dennis Floyd, John Hodge, and David Craig all signed agreements in which they pleaded guilty to one count of money laundering. They were hoping for suspended sentences; none expected prison time.

Then, late that summer, the two remaining big fish—Kelly Campbell and David Ghantt—joined the guilty list.

At a court hearing on September 3, Kelly pleaded guilty to bank larceny and money laundering. She agreed to testify in related trials if asked by prosecutors, who in return dropped a charge of accessory after the fact. After the plea, her lawyer, James Gronquist, blamed his client's involvement in the heist on the "magnetic personality" of Steve Chambers.

A week later, on September 11, Ghantt pleaded guilty to bank larceny and two counts of money laundering. "I regret that I got entangled in circumstances that led to pain to my wife and to my family," he said, his parents and wife watching.

Meanwhile, in Colorado, the Calloways seemed on the verge of criminal success.

During the summer, Jody's mother, Kathy Grigg, traveled to Littleton to visit her son. Kathy was upset over the arrests of her daughter Amy and son-in-law Nathan; the couple had married in April 1998. While talking with Jody about it, Kathy noticed he was worried about something himself.

His revelation flabbergasted Kathy. Jody knew what had happened to Amy. He asked his mother if he should return the money.

"It's too late," Kathy said. "You should just keep it now."

Jody would soon give his mother $28,000 to help her get by.

A month later, Jody told his woodworking partner, Joseph Hamilton, about the real source of the $50,000 he had given him earlier in the year. The two of them drove in Jody's Chevy Tahoe to a storage facility, picked up a large black box, and drove back toward Jody's home in Littleton. There, Jody opened the box, showing Joseph over $1 million worth of ones, fives, tens, and twenties. At first, he said it came from repairing air compressors back in North Carolina. Hamilton did not believe him, and Calloway admitted he had stolen it. He wanted Joseph to help him convert it to new bills.

"I don't want to be involved with this," Joseph said.

"You're already involved," Jody responded. "The fifty grand I gave you? That's Loomis Fargo money. The money orders we've purchased? That was Loomis Fargo money. Whether you want to be involved or not, you're involved."

A week later, Jody turned sinister when he visited Joseph in the woodworking shop. "Have you thought about what we talked about?" he asked.

"I don't want to be involved," Joseph said.

"If you think about saying anything to anybody about any of this," Jody quickly responded, "your family and yourself are dead."

A new defendant charged on November 3, 1998, pleaded guilty the same day she was charged. It was Sally Stowe Abernathy, the locally renowned interior designer who had owned the Cramer Mountain house before Steve and Michele bought it for $635,000. The feds said she broke a law by not filing IRS paperwork—Form 8300, to be precise—required when a business received more than $10,000 in cash, as hers had when Steve and Michele paid approximately $40,000 for interior design work in their new home.

She wore a dark suit to court. She was never actually arrested, having agreed to plead guilty before prosecutors formally charged her.

All told, eighteen of the twenty-one defendants pleaded guilty by early November. And the feds expected Michael and Kim Goodman to become the nineteenth and twentieth.

The twenty-first defendant, Jeffrey Guller, was headed to trial. He was the first attorney in that part of North Carolina ever charged with federal money laundering. While mounds of evidence and Steve's eagerness to reduce his sentence through testimony had led the other defendants to plead guilty and try to move on with their lives, Guller hoped that he could beat the case and not be forced to give up lawyering, which a guilty plea would necessitate. If a jury convicted him, he stood to face more time than some of the money stealers themselves, who, by pleading guilty, qualified for reduced sentences. Guller understood that, but he wanted to avoid conviction and continue his practice.

His colleagues in Gastonia did not know if he was guilty or not, but they weren't surprised he would not accept a plea. In Gaston County's legal community, which he had been part of for thirty years, Guller had a reputation for feistiness, a blunt style, and a steely face that could hold its own in a mobster movie. His previous battles with the law and the State Bar Association had wounded him but never knocked him out.

He was also known for his love of sailing and nature photography, and for cursing more than your average Southern gentleman attorney. Sometimes, when a prosecutor would refuse to let a Guller client plead guilty to a reduced charge, meaning the case was bound for trial, Guller would whip a golf tee from his shirt pocket, hold it in front of the prosecutor's face, and say in a challenging tone, "Tee that motherfucker up! Tee it up!" He would demonstrate this tack to fellow defense attorneys in the courthouse hallway, sticking his arms out like he was gripping a golf club, staring at the ground in front of him, and yelling, "Tee that motherfucker up! Tee it up!"

Of course, when teed up, the federal government can be a huge motherfucker. In November, prosecutors applied more pressure to Guller and the Goodmans—the only three defendants who had not yet pleaded guilty—by adding counts that were not related to any newfound wrongdoing. The defense lawyers complained, to no avail, that the new indictments were unfair intimidation tactics designed to make their clients plead guilty.

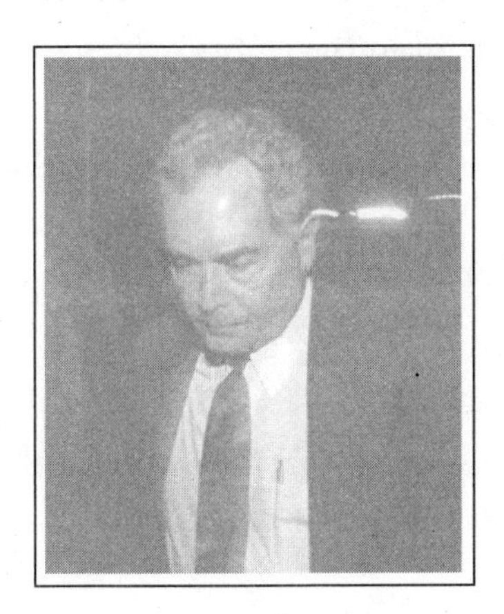

A Revealing Trial

THE TRIAL OF JEFF GULLER began January 4, 1999, seven months after he was originally charged, in a red-carpeted courtroom that sat 120 spectators in six rows of wooden benches. Guller had two of Charlotte's best-known lawyers on his side—Harold Bender, who had defended televangelist Jim Bakker in a famous money-scamming trial in 1988, and Calvin Murphy. The government and Steve Chambers were on the same team for this trial, a result of his agreement to testify. It was the first time the public would see Steve and Kelly speak of their misadventures.

Taking the stand first, Steve recounted his involvement in the heist, sharing familiar details but pinning the ideas for the theft and the murder plot on Kelly. He told the jurors that Guller had first represented him on a larceny charge and that he occasionally asked Guller for advice on matters involving loansharking.

Steve recounted how he brought two bags of cash to Guller's office in the weeks after the heist, intending to use them for the down payment on the $635,000 house. Guller suggested he use checks, he said. Chambers testified about how he retrieved the bags—which contained about $430,000—in early December, after Guller took $10,000 out at Steve's suggestion. When Guller saw the cash, he was "nonchalant," Steve said.

"Why did you leave it with him for that period?" assistant United States attorney Brian Whisler asked.

"I had $14 million," Steve said. "I was looking for somewhere to hide it, so I didn't have a problem with leaving that much with Mr. Guller, as I figured it was a safe place to hide and get rid of a half-million dollars."

Steve also talked about his business ventures.

"Why were you interested in buying a furniture store at this time?" the federal prosecutor asked.

"Me and Mr. Guller had talked about it, as far as would it be good to have a business to run the money through," Steve told the jury. "That way, it wouldn't attract too much attention, as far as cash deposits going into bank accounts."

"Let's be specific," Whisler said. "Who made these statements? Did you make these statements? Or did he make these statements about the purpose of having a business?"

"I'd asked him as far as, 'Would it be better to have a business to run cash money through?' And ultimately, he said, 'Yes, of course.' That way . . . we could put the money into the bank accounts in cash form, and there wouldn't be a lot of questions asked. As far as him coming out and saying, 'You need to go out and buy a business,' no, he did not say that."

Steve discussed the potential deal to buy Crickets. He said he told Guller that he planned to pay the current owner $450,000, some $200,000 of which would be in cash. The paperwork would show the deal being worth $250,000. He testified that they discussed setting up a corporation that would oversee the house, the furniture store, and the nightclub, and that Michele would be president and Guller would be vice president. Steve could not be part of it because his felony conviction would prevent the club from getting a liquor license. That was why he wanted the pardon and why he discussed paying Guller up to $250,000 to get it. The payment would be a bribe, Steve said.

The gist of Steve's testimony was that although he never told Guller about the money's origin, it should have been obvious. At the very least, Steve had made it clear to Guller that he was trying to evade the law, and Guller showed few, if any, qualms about helping him. The details of the deals that never happened—the bribe, for example—did not relate directly to Guller's money-laundering charges, but Judge William Osteen told jurors they could decide from the facts whether there were indications Guller knew Steve's money was dirty.

The government played tapes of conversations between Guller and Steve, including the one in which Guller said he would draw up an agreement reflecting Steve's desire to keep a $20,000 deal with Mike Staley "under the table."

During the cross-examination, Guller attorney Calvin Murphy tried to show the jury that Steve was a lying schemer who was smart enough to con others, including Guller, into believing him.

"I wouldn't say I'm too smart," Steve told Murphy. "If I was, I probably wouldn't be sitting where I'm sitting right now."

After establishing that bookmaking and gambling accounted for two-thirds of Steve's income in the mid-1990s, Murphy asked him to explain his past "occupation." "Now, tell us about bookmaking. What do you do?"

"What do you *do*?"

"Yeah. What is involved?"

"Bookmaking is, people lay bets with you on ball games—football, baseball, basketball. [You] go by the point spread, over and under. Depends on what they want to bet, how much they want to bet, how many teams they want to bet on."

Murphy also had Steve recount the substance of his fraud charges.

Basically, Steve told the jury, he used phony names to open tiny accounts at area banks, after which he cashed phony checks there, then disappeared. In an unrelated tax scam, he made money by filing tax returns under false names.

Murphy also reviewed for the jury the paperwork involving Kelly Campbell's minivan purchase, for which Steve had been present. "Now, on that application, did it ask you for the name of your employer?"

"Yes, it does," Chambers said.

"And what was your response to that?"

"Chambers Industries."

"What is Chambers Industries?"

"I like to call it an industry. It's better than saying Chambers Bookmaking or anything like that. So I come up with Chambers Industries."

Murphy asked about the murder plot. "Do you recall telling Mr. McKinney that he could walk up to Mr. Ghantt with a silencer on the gun and just shoot him and keep walking?"

"Yes, we had that conversation," Steve said.

Murphy ended the cross-examination by noting that Steve's plea bargain allowed him the possibility of a reduced sentence for his government testimony. "Now, tell us, Mr. Chambers, what you would do for your freedom."

"What would I *do*?"

"What acts would you engage in, what conduct would you engage in, for the sake of your freedom?"

"I don't think I follow you here."

"Would you steal for your freedom?"

"Yes, I probably would."

"Would you lie for your freedom?"

"Yes, I probably would."

"Would you deceive for your freedom?"

"Yes, I probably would."

"But today," Murphy deadpanned, "you have been truthful, correct?"

"Yes, I have."

During further questioning, Whisler asked Steve to explain why he assumed Guller knew the source of the money.

"When I called Mr. Guller up to help Kelly out as far as the FBI questioning her about a polygraph test, I had spoken to Mr. Guller about that. That was right in the first week of October, after Kelly had been interviewed after the robbery. And Mr. Guller had said that he would handle the case for her. I paid him $500 down to talk to the FBI, to keep the FBI away from her. Kelly went to be interviewed by Mr. Guller. And then, of course, later on, I ended up purchasing the $635,000 home."

"Anything else?"

"Well, it just led me to believe that Mr. Guller knew where the funds came from. I don't think it took a rocket scientist to figure that out. That's my opinion."

Kelly Campbell was the next government witness. Federal prosecutor David Keesler started off by having her acknowledge her frequent marijuana use before her arrest, and how it had affected her memory of events.

She recounted how Steve, after the heist, introduced her to Guller, who called the FBI for her when she told him agents wanted her to take a polygraph.

During the cross-examination, when Harold Bender asked Kelly to recount more details of the heist planning, she said the theft was Steve's idea, contradicting Steve, who had pinned that responsibility on her.

"Steve Chambers was the brains? The mastermind?"

"Yes."

"Steve Chambers called the shots?"

"Yes, he did. . . . He made all of the plans of how the money was going to be taken care of, where it was going to be hid. He had control of all the money. He made all of the plans as to how to carry it out. He said who got what."

Perhaps worried that the government's two witnesses had contradicted each other, David Keesler asked Kelly more about her pot use.

She started smoking it around age thirteen, she said. At the time of the crime, she was smoking about three joints a day. "It got to a point where I was smoking pot like most people smoke cigarettes," she said.

"Just a minute," the judge said. "When you say, 'Like most people smoke cigarettes,' I don't really know whether most people smoke cigarettes or not, but assuming they do, what do you mean by that?"

Kelly said, "When I'd get up in the morning, I would smoke a joint. If I was going to go shopping, I had to smoke a joint. I felt like I couldn't function unless I was stoned."

Jennifer Norman, Guller's former office assistant, took the stand next. She told the jurors that she and the office secretary grew suspicious after learning Steve and Michele wanted to buy the $635,000 house, because Guller had just represented Steve on the fraudulent-check charges. Then, when she saw Steve's bags of money, she was certain it came from the Loomis Fargo heist. She said she told Guller her feelings, even mentioning the reward on *America's Most Wanted*, but that Guller said she could not prove it was Loomis money.

After a few more questions from Whisler, she said this: "He told me that he didn't really care where the money came from. He was getting paid. And in the law office, I mean, he let a lot of people finance out—you know, pay down and whatever. And Steve was always one to pay up front, and so his comment was, 'I don't care. I get paid.' Because like I said, Steve was always one to pay up front. He paid his bill."

Norman also told jurors how she called *America's Most Wanted* but was basically blown off, because the only suspect at that time was David Ghantt.

In the cross-examination, Murphy had Norman acknowledge that she lacked legal or paralegal training, and that Guller had never discussed *any* attorney-client conversations with her; therefore, his not talking to her about Steve Chambers was insignificant.

The next witness was John Hodge, the sixty-nine-year-old father of Calvin Hodge. Both father and son had pleaded guilty to money laundering. John Hodge spoke in an extremely high-pitched voice. He seemed proud at being part of such a distinguished courtroom setting, even as he recounted his deeds of questionable repute.

He told the jury how Steve Chambers contacted him after the heist about securing a $100,000 check for him. Steve wanted the check to

Lawyers for Jeff Guller (*center*) tried to impeach the credibility of Steve Chambers, the government's main witness.
Jeff Siner / CHARLOTTE OBSERVER

buy his house. He would give Hodge that amount in cash, plus a fee, and Hodge would take the money out of his personal checking account to make out the check. Hodge refused to get Steve the $100,000 check but agreed to get him one for $80,000. Steve paid him a 10 percent fee that equaled $8,000. Soon after that, he asked Hodge to secure another check, this one for $62,000, for Steve's mobile-home purchase. Hodge's fee was 10 percent for this check also, bringing his total in fees to $14,200.

Keesler asked, "What did you think about the fact that Mr. Chambers was going to pay you money to go get these checks?"

"Well," Hodge told the jurors, "years ago, I used to be what you call a speculator and a '10 percenter,' if any of you is familiar with either one of them. And that's where you would do something, and they would pay you 10 percent for doing it, and that was my purpose of doing the transaction is the 10 percent, and not knowing any more about the situation than what it was. But I personally wouldn't do it again under the circumstances, any circumstances."

Several courtroom observers chuckled to themselves. If the jury had not been watching, Keesler probably would have covered his face with his hands.

After a brief cross-examination, Hodge asked the judge if he could stay in the courtroom and watch the next witness, his son Calvin, who told the jury about his money laundering and about the $40,000 Steve paid him to open a safe-deposit box.

The witness who followed Calvin Hodge, FBI agent Bart Boodee, talked about his interviews with Guller on the days of the first heist arrests. He told how Guller changed his story about the cash sitting in his office after Boodee mentioned that lying to the FBI was a felony. Boodee said that, at first, Guller told the FBI the cash was in his office only briefly. But then, after Boodee's "reminder," he said that in fact it was there for weeks, and that before he was to give it back, Steve told him to withdraw some money as a gratuity for holding it. Guller at first declined the offer but finally partook, taking $10,000 for himself, he told Boodee.

John Wydra was the final prosecution witness. The agent summarized the government's case. Using an elaborate computer display shown on a screen for the jury, he outlined the transactions Guller performed or discussed performing for Steve—the house purchase, the mobile-home purchase, the furniture-store purchase, the land deal with Kelly Campbell, and the Crickets deal and its related pardon payoff. Guller's lawyers fumed when Wydra included the deals that never happened—the nightclub, the pardon, the property for Kelly's husband—with those that did. All told, Wydra showed the jury a figure of $1.2 million that "Chambers had available to him with Guller's knowledge."

Wydra also presented the toll records of dozens of calls between Guller's office and Steve's home from October 8, 1997, to February 28, 1998. This led Judge Osteen to remind the jurors that the listing of a person's phone number on a toll record did not necessarily mean that person had placed the call. Calvin Murphy seized on this point as well, noting that busy signals or non-answers appeared on toll records as calls, and that not every call made correlated to a conversation, let alone a conversation about criminal activity.

After the government finished presenting evidence, Guller's lawyers tried to have the case dismissed on technical grounds. They questioned, for example, whether prosecutors had explicitly stated that the money stolen from Loomis Fargo was insured by the Federal Deposit Insurance Corporation, a requirement for the federal charges to apply. Wydra had said that 95 percent of the stolen money belonged to banks, which would qualify, but no paper proof was presented. The judge denied the motion, and the defense started calling witnesses.

One of the first was Lurie Limbaugh, the victim of Steve's theft in 1994. During his testimony, Steve had downplayed the charge as a drug deal gone bad, but the defense wanted to prove he was lying, and also that he was an easy person to trust. Limbaugh said she had met Steve at a Gastonia club, and that he said he could help her buy a car. When she took him up on his offer, she told him she had $3,000 in her purse. While they were parked in a vehicle, he grabbed the money and ran away, she said.

If Limbaugh had trusted Steve enough to be alone with him with $3,000 after having met him just once or twice, the defense attorneys seemed to be asking, couldn't Guller have believed that the much greater sums came from legal gambling proceeds?

Next on the witness stand was a well-known figure in Charlotte, former mayor Richard Vinroot. Vinroot and Guller were childhood friends who attended the same public schools, college, and law school. They were co-captains of the high-school football team. "My opinion is that he has the highest integrity," Vinroot told jurors.

During the cross-examination, Keesler asked, "Mr. Vinroot, you don't know anything about the underlying facts of this case, do you?"

"Absolutely nothing about it," the former mayor said. "I have, frankly, not kept up with it because I was so hurt by the allegations, of course, and worried about my friend."

Keesler asked him if he knew that, in the past, the State Bar Association had reprimanded Guller for unrelated matters involving his legal practice.

"No, sir, I was not aware of that," Vinroot said, adding that he and Guller had infrequent contact the last ten to fifteen years.

Next, two of Guller's Gaston County colleagues, Max Childers and Calvin Hamrick—the latter a former district attorney—told jurors they thought Guller had integrity, though they admitted knowing little, if anything, of his state-bar reprimands.

Guller's wife, Brenda, took the stand next and said Jeff was a very good stepfather to her children from a previous marriage.

The defense's most important witness was Guller himself. He took the stand after his wife, on Thursday, January 7, 1999. Calvin Murphy started by asking him about his background. Guller spoke of his 1966 law degree from the University of North Carolina at Chapel Hill, his work as a prosecutor in the late 1960s, his six months of active duty in the National Guard, and his leadership roles in the Gaston County March of Dimes, the Red Cross, the Young Lawyers Association, and his synagogue.

He related to jurors that he met Steve Chambers in 1995, to discuss the 1994 larceny charge. Steve told him he worked in Charlotte and made $11.50 an hour at a company named Hydrovac, where he had allegedly been employed for six years. Guller had no reason not to believe him, he said. On Steve's next date before the bench, which came on November 17, 1995, Guller went to court but Steve did not show up, and the judge issued a warrant for his arrest.

The next time Steve and Guller met was twenty months later, when Steve went to see him about the worthless-check charges.

"What was his attitude when he came to see you?" Murphy asked.

"He seemed a little put out with me about the larceny warrant, about why I didn't get it handled," Guller testified. "I got a little put out with him and said, 'Where the hell were you? I can't deal with your case unless you come to court, and I'm not going to deal with your case unless you pay me.' "

"What was his response or reaction to that?"

"He said, 'Fine, fine, we will work everything out,' and I said okay."

Murphy asked, "Did he ever talk to you about bookmaking, loansharking, gambling, anything like that?"

"Never, other than the fact about his Atlantic City [trips]," Guller said.

He told about the deal for the $635,000 house and the bag containing

$433,000 that Chambers brought to the closing. Guller told him that they would need to take the money to the bank and fill out forms reporting the source of the funds. "He didn't appear to want to do that," Guller told the jury. "I said, 'Why not?' I said, 'If it's valid money, if you won it like you said, it's already reported, so why not?' "

Guller testified about how he told Chambers to bring him other funds, and soon, or they would have to put the cash in the bank, since they were closing on the house. He also said he asked Chambers how he could afford the house. "He said that he had won a great deal of money gambling in Atlantic City," Guller testified.

Murphy asked, "Did you pursue that any further with him?"

"I did. I asked him how much he won, and he didn't say. He just said, 'A lot of money, more than enough to buy this house.' "

Guller testified that he had no reason to suspect Steve was involved with the Loomis heist. "This thing was reported as maybe the second-biggest robbery in the United States. Chambers? No way did Chambers have sense enough to do something like this. . . . I had no idea what he won in Atlantic City."

Steve eventually brought Guller checks to pay for the house, so Guller never had to deposit the $433,000 in the bank. But he acknowledged taking $10,000 from the bag before returning it. He said Steve told him to take the money several times before he agreed, and that he did so only because Steve said it was a Christmas gift. "[Chambers] called me and said, 'Things went real well, and I appreciate what you did.' I said, 'Fine, thank you.' He said, 'I want you to take $10,000.' And I said, 'No, I'm not taking $10,000.' He said, 'I want you to take $10,000.' I said, 'We'll see.' So I didn't do anything. He called me another time and said, 'Have you taken your $10,000?' And I said no. 'I want you to take $10,000.' I said, 'Okay, we'll see.' And I didn't. And when he called and asked for the money back, he said, 'Have you taken your $10,000?' I said no. He said, 'I want you to take $10,000.' He said, 'Christmas is coming, take the $10,000.' I said okay."

Then he recounted the proposed land deal involving Kelly

Campbell's husband, in which Guller said he would help Steve put the land under a phony name. In giving his testimony, Guller unwittingly riled the judge.

Murphy asked, "Did you ever tell [Steve] that you could put it in a fictitious name?"

"I may have said 'Yeah' or 'Okay,' just to get him off the phone."

"Did you have any intentions of doing that?"

"Absolutely not. I wouldn't do that for anybody."

"Did he ever bring any specific documents to you . . . ?"

"Just a minute," Judge Osteen interrupted, facing Guller. "Why would you have said that to get him off the phone?"

"A lot of times," Guller said, "when I'm talking to somebody, a client or whoever, and he's told me what he needed to tell me, that he wanted me to do some work, and then he just starts talking, and I have got another line holding or I have got somewhere else I've got to be or I've got something else to do, I just want to be off the phone."

His answer appalled the judge. "Isn't he, at that time, asking you about some legal advice? 'Will you put it in an assumed name?' That's legal advice he is asking you for, isn't it?"

Guller said, "I think I've gotten the gist of what he wanted to say by then, and that was an opportunity where he just took to talk, and he liked to talk big about things that he could do."

"All right, sir," the judge said. "Proceed, Mr. Murphy."

Murphy proceeded to finish up the direct examination. Guller said the alleged bribe for Steve's pardon would have been simply a fee to an attorney who specialized in getting pardons.

During this testimony, the defense couldn't get to what Guller felt was the heart of the issue—that attorneys like the pardon maker, who once worked in government, had developed influence with public officials that they could charge other people money to use. Evidence to support that point would surely be inadmissible.

Keesler, in perhaps the most devastating part of his cross-examination, insinuated that Guller must have been an absolute dolt not to realize the source of Steve's money. Citing the testimony of Jennifer Norman, who had called *America's Most Wanted*, he reminded Guller—and the jurors—that Norman had considerably less formal education than he did. "You have a college and law degree, don't you?" Keesler asked.

"Yes, sir," Guller said.

"And you're a practicing lawyer for thirty years?"

"Yes."

"And none of this clicked for you, I take it?"

"No, sir."

"You didn't see anything unusual about it at all."

"No, sir."

During his closing argument to the jurors, Harold Bender said Guller simply did not know where the money came from. "If his client lies to him, how is he supposed to know? If Mr. Guller's client says, 'I won a whole lot of money in Atlantic City,' does Mr. Guller say, 'I don't believe you. Get out of my office'?"

As for Steve Chambers, Bender said, "There's not a truthful bone in that man's body. He involved his parents. He involved his in-laws. He involved his friends. He's a user. He's a manipulator. He's the government's primary witness."

Parts of Guller's testimony could have inspired reasonable doubt against the government's case, if the jurors believed his point of view. But he seemed uncooperative to the prosecutor on the witness stand and appeared to be lying when he said he did not suspect Steve was involved in the heist. And on the tapes, he sounded like an aider and abetter to Chambers; at the very least, he sounded indifferent.

The jury took just four hours in the late afternoon on January 8, 1999, to send back guilty verdicts against him.

Selling Elvis, and the Colorado Connection

PUBLIC WONDERMENT OVER THE HEIST was such that, on February 20, 1999, about five thousand people crowded the Metrolina Expo flea market for the government's auction of seized items bought with heist loot. Typically, federal auctions of criminals' seized possessions are low-profile, but this one drew newspapers, *People* magazine, and network TV crews. Publicity before the auction was strong. People had called from across the country asking about the velvet Elvis, which had become a symbol of the heist's wackiness, despite the inaccuracy of the common belief that it had hung prominently in Steve and Michele's house. The Elvis, minus the context, was worth about $30, but the auctioneer expected it to bring as much as $1,000. It was one of many attention-grabbing items up for sale, competing with a blue barrel used to store money, Michele's convertible BMW, a silver cigar holder engraved with the name of Steve Chambers, statues, paintings, and the six-foot wooden Indian.

The scattered laughter increased when Manny Fisher, the bespectacled, gray-haired auctioneer, announced that the blue barrel was up for bid. Like the velvet Elvis, it was worth maybe $30 brand new but was clearly going to fetch more—perhaps $100, some speculated, or $150 if someone was feeling loony.

Bidding for the barrel shot up to $500 in less than thirty seconds, thrilling the crowd, whose disbelief gave way to guffaws, then to unified laughter. The bids kept rising—$600, then $700. Even Fisher, who expected some antics, could not believe how high the bids were going. Eight hundred dollars, then $900, then, finally, $1,050 from the owner of a Charlotte recycling company. She would place it proudly in her front office.

The crowd cheered when Fisher held up the velvet Elvis. People shook their heads as the bids shot past $1,200, then $1,300, then $1,500. It finally sold for $1,600 to Tom Shaw, the owner of the American Gun and Pawn Shop on South Boulevard, where it would hang for publicity purposes. Shaw received a certificate of authenticity that the piece was a "seized asset from the $17 million Loomis Fargo robbery."

Most people at the auction spent lesser amounts on small statues, paintings, or knickknacks from Steve and Michele's house or on furniture seized from their store. The owner of a publicity company spent $32,000 on Michele's BMW, about $1,500 less than it was worth. He planned to donate it to a children's charity he owned, which would raffle it off. Eric Payne's Harley-Davidson sold for $16,000.

In all, the auction raised $360,000. It was destined for Loomis Fargo and its insurance company, Lloyd's of London.

Two months earlier, Steve and Michele's criminally acquired house had sold for $486,000, to a doctor, his wife, and their children.

On January 20, 1999, Philip Noel Johnson was sentenced to twenty-five years in prison for stealing $18.8 million from Loomis Fargo in Florida and holding up his colleagues at gunpoint twenty-two months earlier.

The defendants in the North Carolina heist expected far less time behind bars, because they did not use, or threaten to use, weapons during the theft. Technically, they did not rob anybody, since robbery involves the use or threat of force. No one, therefore, was charged with robbery; instead, the defendants were charged mostly with bank larceny, which carried a maximum sentence of ten years, in addition to money laundering, which had a maximum sentence of twenty years. Their guilty pleas and—generally speaking—insignificant prior criminal records would increase their odds of receiving sentences far lighter than the maximum.

Still, they were nervous. On February 23, 1999, six of the defendants walked into the federal courthouse on Trade Street to learn their punishments. Perusing a paper sentencing grid that used current and past convictions as a guide for each crime, Judge Graham Mullen sentenced Scott Grant to four years and seven months in prison and ordered him to pay $26,000 in restitution. The judge sentenced Eric Payne, who had spent much more heist money than Grant, to six and a half years in prison and ordered him to pay $292,000 in restitution. A portion of whatever money they made when freed would go to Loomis Fargo and its insurance company, until both were fully reimbursed.

"Mr. Payne, I realize there's probably no way on God's green earth you can pay back $292,000," Judge Mullen told him. "The law requires that I impose that."

"I made a bad mistake," Payne said. "And Lord knows, I would take it back."

The longest sentence of the day, eleven years and three months, went to Mike McKinney. The shortest sentences went to Sandra Floyd, Dennis Floyd, and Calvin Hodge. Each received three years of probation. In addition, Hodge was sentenced to spend four months under house arrest and to perform a hundred hours of community service.

Michele Chambers came to court to watch her parents' sentencing. She knew they would not have been there if not for her. Michele cried and hugged her sister when Mullen announced probation instead of prison for the Floyds, who held each other's hands as the judge spoke. Prosecutor Brian Whisler told the judge the Floyds had been the most forthcoming of all the defendants in the case.

The next day, two more defendants—John Hodge and David Craig—each received two years of probation on their money-laundering charges. Craig was also sentenced to six months of work release and six months of house arrest. Hodge's lawyer, James Gray, cracked up the courtroom when he revealed that his client actually declared as income on his tax return the $14,200 that Chambers paid him to launder money. After the court hearing, Hodge told the *Charlotte Observer*

This seemingly ordinary barrel, where stolen money was hidden under dog food, drew a $1,050 bid at an auction of the defendants' seized possessions.
CHARLOTTE OBSERVER

he considered it a "service" to buy the checks for Chambers. "I didn't have any reason to doubt that it [was] legitimate money," he said. "Nowadays, you never know who has $100,000 or $150,000 available."

The search continued for the missing $2.6 million.

Lloyd's of London had on the case an investigative firm called Amsec International, which had an investigator named Joel Bartow, who spent weeks at a time in North Carolina interviewing defendants about the whereabouts of the money. His job could be dirty. Sometimes, he drove outside the homes of Michele Chambers and the Floyds, took their roadside garbage bags, put them in his trunk, and drove elsewhere to examine them. He tried the same tactic outside the home of Robert and Mary Chambers, but every time he drove nearby, they came to the window, and his cover was blown. He discovered paperwork that indicated Michele Chambers had rented a storage facility that the FBI did not know about, but it turned out to have nothing special inside, just a few inexpensive household goods.

During his interviews, he came across Dennis Floyd, who, when pressed, said his stepdaughter Michele had some jewelry hidden in the house. Shortly thereafter, the FBI recovered the $43,000 diamond ring, after Bartow and Floyd persuaded Michele that returning it was in everybody's interest. When Michele handed it to John Wydra at the FBI's Charlotte headquarters, the agent asked, without skipping a beat, "Where's the Rolex?" She answered that she had sold it. She also returned the diamond tennis bracelet.

Though she had hidden her jewelry, prosecutors did not immediately push to revoke Michele's bond. That changed on March 8, 1999, when the FBI arrested her while she was working at Chili's. Michele may have still loved Steve, but while he sat in jail, she met a new man. A string of incidents involving this new boyfriend, a local bartender, got her back in trouble.

At a court hearing the day after the new arrest, the United States

Probation Office offered seven reasons her bond should be revoked. The most obvious was how she concealed the $43,000 ring. But what spurred the government to lock her up again stemmed from an anonymous call to the FBI on December 29, 1998, reporting that she was drinking excessively at the Graduate Pub in Gastonia and waving a gun in the parking lot. On January 7, 1999, a probation officer told her to get rid of the stun gun she carried. That officer also informed her that a handgun carried by her bartender boyfriend could get her in trouble. Then, on February 17, Gastonia police had arrived at the bartender's home after neighbors complained of a loud argument there. When the officers knocked on the door and identified themselves, the bartender threatened to shoot them. The apartment door opened, and Michele came outside. The bartender then approached the door holding a pistol. He quickly put it down but was charged with communicating threats.

Michele had violated several bond conditions, the government argued—by drinking excessively, by associating with a person involved in unlawful conduct, and by not following her probation officer's instructions.

Her lawyer, Andy Culler, said Michele should not be penalized for her boyfriend's behavior, but he did not strongly contest the government's request. Judge Horn returned Michele to jail on March 11. At the hearing, Culler asked the judge to ensure that, while in jail, Michele receive medication for back pain, anxiety, and depression.

The hubbub led to the postponement of her sentencing until later in 1999.

On March 29, two other defendants were sentenced. Steve's parents, convicted of money laundering for renting safe-deposit boxes, learned that they would stay out of prison but be confined to their home for five months. After the house arrest, they each would have to serve two years and seven months of probation. It was a more severe sentence than that given to Michele's parents, who each got off with just probation.

"They don't deserve prison," said David Phillips, the lawyer for Steve's parents. "They still love their son, even though their son got them in trouble."

On April 27, Amy Grant—formerly Amy Grigg, before her marriage to Nathan about a year earlier—was sentenced to eighteen months in prison, with the option of shortening it to six months if she served it in a prison boot camp. The judge, scheduled to sentence Nathan Grant two days later, agreed to stagger their sentences so that one of them could always be living with their children; they had welcomed their second child a month earlier.

In 1976, a few months after French master thief Albert Spaggiari led the $8 million Nice bank theft and treated his associates to an elegant meal in the vault, members of his gang confessed, and he was captured. Every Thursday for several weeks, he was questioned in a second-floor room in the courthouse. On March 10, 1977, after complaining of the heat and walking toward the window, Spaggiari jumped outside. Shocked investigators and guards ran to the window just in time to see Spaggiari, a former paratrooper, skillfully land on a car roof and hop on the back of a waiting motorcycle, which drove him away. He was not seen again until his death in 1989—when his body was delivered to his mother's house—though he did send money to the car owner for damage to the roof, and he occasionally mailed reporters postcards to show he was still alive. Less than $250,000 of the stolen money has been recovered.

David Ghantt and Steve Chambers, led into court in prison garb and shackles on April 29, 1999, for sentencing, attempted no such theatrics.

Steve read an apology from a piece of paper. "I wish I could take back that October night, but I can't," he said. "I don't know if I can get over the hurt I've caused my children from being greedy. . . . I lost sight of what's important in life, which are hugs and kisses from my kids."

Before his testimony had helped the prosecution, Steve Chambers figured on getting fifteen to nineteen years in prison. Prosecutor Brian Whisler told Judge Mullen that the government now recommended a lesser sentence—eleven years and three months. "We believe his testimony was helpful to secure the government conviction of Mr. Guller at the trial," he told the judge.

But Steve Chambers thought he deserved an even lighter sentence for confessing right after his arrests, pleading guilty, and testifying against Guller. Chris Fialko, his lawyer, pushed for a seven-and-a-half-year sentence.

The judge sided with the prosecutor, opting for the same sentence given to Mike McKinney. The judge also ordered Steve to pay $3.8 million in restitution.

Outside the courthouse, Fialko told reporters that "Steve believes in the future, when there's a big case, the big defendants will not have as much incentive to cooperate, because the government did not give him as much of a reduction as he felt he deserves."

After sentencing Steve Chambers, Judge Mullen listened to David Ghantt's statement. Ghantt stood up and stuck out his chest as if concerned about displaying proper posture. The judge smiled. "Your Honor, if I could undo what I did, I would," David said. "I see how I hurt my wife and my family. I'm sorry for what I did. I was stuck in a go-nowhere job. . . . I was unhappy with my life. I worked a lot of hours. It's no excuse for what I did. I'm sorry."

Judge Mullen sentenced David to seven and a half years in prison and the payment of $3.8 million in restitution. It was no surprise he received less time than Steve, who had much more control of the stolen money after the theft and who, after all, plotted to kill David.

Nobody expected that David Ghantt, Kelly Campbell, or Steve Chambers would ever pay off their restitution. They would be lucky if more of the missing money was found or if the others found a way to pay it off. Then they would no longer be liable for it. But they were likely to have to write restitution checks for the rest of their lives.

During the same court session in which Ghantt and Chambers were sentenced, Judge Mullen sentenced Nathan Grant to three years and one month in prison and Amy Payne to a year of work release plus two years of probation. Each would also pay restitution.

The family atmosphere in the courtroom was strong that day. Nine defendants were present: David Ghantt, Steve Chambers, his parents, Amy Payne, Eric Payne, Amy Grant, Nathan Grant, and Scott Grant, who, like Eric Payne, had not been sent to prison yet.

When Steve settled into the defendant's seat and looked around the courtroom, he made eye contact with Scott Grant in one of the spectator rows. He nodded at Scott, the way people who are close nod at each other.

Scott held Steve largely responsible for his fate. He did not expect any such gesture from Steve and certainly did not want to show him support, but, not catching himself, he nodded back. Seconds later, he was disgusted he had not just looked away.

In June and September, two people were sentenced who, in retrospect, could have gotten lesser penalties.

Jeff Guller received eight years in prison, a heavier punishment than that given to the person who actually stole the money.

"I will survive, and I will be back," Guller said in court. "And I will be a citizen of this country that works hard and . . . accomplishes something." He said he rued the day Steve Chambers first came into his office. "I'm not a money launderer," Guller said. "Nor would I ever conspire with a thief like him."

The North Carolina State Bar dealt with Guller's situation in the summer, disbarring him, to nobody's surprise.

Also to nobody's surprise, given her recent bond revocation,

Michele Chambers was sentenced in September to seven years and eight months in prison—the fourth-most-severe sentence in the case, after Steve's, Mike McKinney's, and Guller's. She was also ordered to pay $4.8 million in restitution. Judge Mullen recommended she receive mental-health treatment in prison.

Mullen settled on Michele's sentence as a compromise. The government wanted a nine-year sentence, and Michele's lawyer suggested seven years and three months. Andy Culler told the judge his client had endured a difficult personal life because of her parents' divorce, a teenage pregnancy, and various medical conditions. But Brian Whisler told the court her personal history was irrelevant. "There are many people with those factors who don't resort to crime," he said.

The last main defendant to be sentenced, Kelly Campbell, got five years and ten months, which was less than David Ghantt or Steve Chambers received. She was ordered to pay $4.7 million in restitution.

Kelly cried at the hearing and apologized for her crimes. She now realized, she said, that religion and family were more important than money. "I'd gotten too far away from the Lord, and He had to do something to wake me up," Kelly told Judge Mullen.

Mullen said, "It's always refreshing to the court to hear someone fess up and take their medicine." He ordered that her sentence not begin until January 2000, so she could spend Christmas at home with her children—under house arrest.

New Year's Eve and the first months of 2000 brought little change in the case; each of the twenty-one defendants had already been convicted and sentenced. The FBI had a full slate of new crimes to investigate. John Wydra and the other agents moved on to other cases, relegating the Loomis heist to almost a hobby status. Though Loomis cash was still missing, the FBI felt it had better ways to spend taxpayer money

About 18 months after jokingly mugging for the camera the day of her arrest, Kelly Campbell (*front*) had a more serious tone when she learned her sentence.
CHARLOTTE OBSERVER

than by devoting its limited staff to completing what was, from the agency's perspective, a puzzle that was largely solved.

Wydra was still hoping to find the money unaccounted for, which was believed, after further reviews of assets, to be approximately $1.5 million.

He had secured a list of names of everybody with accounts at Lincoln Self Storage, from which Steve Chambers said the missing money had disappeared. He noticed something special about the name Jennifer Calloway. A records search revealed she had once shared an address with Nathan and Amy Grant, both of whom had admitted hiding Steve's stolen money at Lincoln Self Storage. But the normal course of new cases coming its way left the FBI little time to investigate the match.

Of course, the victim companies—Loomis Fargo and its insurance company, Lloyd's of London—desperately wanted the money found. Lloyd's was still paying Amsec International to try to find the cash. The people at Amsec figured the FBI now had higher crime-fighting priorities, so they stepped up their own efforts.

Robert Osborne, Jr., of Amsec interviewed Michele and Steve Chambers in prison, separately, to check their credibility on the Lincoln Self Storage theft. Both mentioned Nathan Grant as having helped them stash the money that was now missing.

Osborne wanted to travel to Beckley, West Virginia, to talk to both Grant brothers, who were in prison there. He had trouble gaining access because he wasn't a law-enforcement officer. The FBI helped arrange his clearance.

Before Osborne had a chance to talk with the Grants, a prison official shocked him with the revelation that months earlier, another inmate had mentioned that one of the Grant boys had been bragging that he had money waiting for him when he left prison—money from the heist. The inmate thought that sharing the information would win him time off his sentence. But until Osborne's trip, nobody passed it on.

On August 10, 2000, Nathan Grant told Osborne that his wife's half-brother, Jody Calloway, supposedly had the missing money. Amsec now had the name. For more information, Osborne needed to talk to Amy Grant and her mother, Kathy Grigg.

On August 23, Osborne and another Amsec employee, Jamie Waters, arrived at Amy and Kathy's home in Maiden, North Carolina. Amy was there. Osborne and Waters announced themselves as investigators interested only in finding the money, not in prosecuting her, and said they would make a positive recommendation to the government if Amy was helpful.

Her mother was at a doctor's appointment, Amy told them. But yes, she knew about the money. Her mother had told her, during the summer of 1998, that Jody Calloway had it. Her mother knew more about it than Amy, but Amy had a few details of her own to provide, details that helped implicate Jody. She said the amount of cash that she and Nathan hid for Steve Chambers scared her so much that she told Jody, her half-brother, that she was storing money for the mob. She told him the money was at Lincoln Self Storage, in case anything happened to her. A receipt from the storage facility lying around her home might have led the Calloways to the locker, Amy indicated. If the investigators wanted more, they needed to speak to her mother, who Amy had to pick up at the doctor's.

That night, after Kathy Grigg arrived, Osborne told her, as he had told her daughter, that Amsec was interested only in recovering the money. Kathy then added essential details. Yes, Jody and Jennifer Calloway had lived with the Grants, but they moved to Colorado a few months after the heist. Yes, Jody took the stolen money from the storage locker. He had admitted it to her. Kathy told Osborne how Jody had asked if he should return the money, how she had told him to just keep it, and how Jody had given her $28,000 in cash when he visited her months later in North Carolina. Kathy felt bad, like she was betraying her son. She told the two investigators that she hoped her cooperation would count toward Jody's benefit.

Both women gave written statements.

Amsec called the FBI. Five days later, Osborne and Wydra went to the home and had Kathy read back her statement to double-check its veracity. She told them it was true.

Next, the FBI made plans to visit Jody in Colorado. The agents would try to use his half-sister against him. Having pleaded guilty to money laundering and now serving probation, Amy agreed to help the government.

At this point, the main direct evidence against the Calloways was the word of Jody's mother, but circumstantial evidence was growing. Records showed they lived in a $212,000 home, a considerable improvement on their accommodations in North Carolina. Employment tax records showed Jody Calloway had earned $608 during the second quarter of 1998 and $731 during the fourth quarter of 1999. Jennifer Calloway hadn't made much more. Yet according to Department of Motor Vehicle records, they owned five vehicles—a 1998 Ford Explorer, a 1996 Chevy Tahoe, a 1985 Ford Mustang, a 1977 Harley-Davidson, and a 1990 Chris-Craft power boat.

On August 31, 2000, the FBI secretly videotaped a meeting between Amy and Jody in a Colorado hotel room.

Amy told him their mother had told her about Jody's theft of heist money.

Jody angrily denied everything and told her he bet the FBI was watching him as he spoke. He also said their mother was crazy.

Amy advised him to return the money, to think of the family.

"I don't know nothin' about this bullshit!" Jody yelled. "You need to stop insinuating that I do!"

Jody did not confess, but the FBI felt confident enough about the circumstantial evidence and about Calloway's angry mood with Amy Grant that Wydra arrested him later in the day. In court, a federal magistrate ordered him kept in custody in Englewood, Colorado, without bond. The judge instructed United States marshals to transport him to Charlotte to face the federal charge of possession of stolen property. He was subsequently taken to jail in Charlotte, where circumstantial evidence was building further against both him and his wife, Jennifer.

On October 2, 2000, Brian Whisler found himself in court again, to argue at a bond hearing in a case the government nicknamed "Loomis II." Whisler told Magistrate-Judge Brent McKnight that Calloway should be kept in jail without bond. He cited the move to Colorado, Calloway's failure to list most of his vehicles on a financial disclosure form after his arrest, and his alleged propensity toward violence. Calloway had been recently charged with felony menacing in Colorado for an alleged road-rage incident involving a gun.

Jody's attorney, Chuck Morgan, contended that the government's evidence was flimsy, and that hard work and savings were responsible for the couple's Colorado lifestyle.

Judge McKnight decided to free Jody Calloway on $150,000 bond, putting him under house arrest in Littleton, Colorado. He ordered Jody to get a job.

Meanwhile, back in Charlotte, a federal grand jury met in November and indicted him for money laundering, his wife for possession of stolen property and money laundering, and his mother for possession of stolen property—the $28,000 she said Calloway had given her.

The next month, John Wydra appeared before judges and was granted warrants to seize the Calloways' five vehicles and Wells Fargo bank account and to search their residence, 5586 West Rowland Place in Littleton.

On March 5, Wydra seized boxes of paperwork from the home, including pay stubs from Riviera Electric, where Jody had worked, credit-card statements, closing documents on the home, receipts, financial notes, bills, business cards, titles to their vehicles, and their tax returns for 2000.

On March 13, Wydra tried to seize money from the Wells Fargo bank account, only to learn that Jennifer Calloway had emptied it of $52,000 earlier in the day. He secured another warrant for it.

Jennifer eventually turned the money over to the government on May 8.

Tammy Ghantt decided it was time to move on. About a year after David was sentenced, she filed for divorce. Their reconciliation following his arrest had not erased the pain of his abandonment, and she wanted to get on with her life without him.

There was nothing David could do but accept her decision. Imprisoned in Butner, North Carolina, he took classes to learn a trade. He planned to be an electrician when freed.

Kelly Campbell, incarcerated in Alderson, West Virginia, took classes to become a welder. She reconciled with her husband and lost twenty pounds.

Michele Chambers, also at Alderson, took classes to become a paralegal. Her goal was to support her kids on her own when freed.

The trial of Jody and Jennifer Calloway began August 20, 2001. On its first day, government witness Steve Chambers spoke about paying Nathan Grant and Amy Grigg, Nathan's then-girlfriend, $70,000 in return for their help hiding millions of dollars at Lincoln Self Storage. Only the three of them had keys to the locker, Steve testified. He recounted how, in December 1997, they had discovered that the key did not work and that the money was missing.

Confusion reigned on the trial's second day when Kathy Grigg, the government's star witness, directly contradicted everything she had told Amsec and the FBI when they visited her house the previous August. Her words baffled the prosecutors because they had offered her immunity for her truthful testimony. Challenged by the angry prosecutors about the written statement she had signed thirteen months earlier, she mystified them by saying her son had never told her he stole the money and had never given her $28,000. In Kathy's words, when Amsec officials came to her house, "I was frightened and scared, so I told them it was true." She described her medical problems, which included high blood pressure and depression, and said she was sedated during the Amsec interview, having just returned from her doctor. "I wasn't aware of what I was writing when I wrote it," she said.

That afternoon, as court was closing down, Jody Calloway glared at Joseph Hamilton, who was scheduled to testify the next day. Hamilton, Jody's business partner in Colorado, was also Jennifer Calloway's brother-in-law. Jody's glare frightened Hamilton enough that he wondered what would happen if Jody were free. He knew what he had to do.

On the next day, his surprise testimony made the trial's outcome a virtual certainty. In a confession with the jurors out of the courtroom, Hamilton told the judge that in 1998, Jody Calloway had shown him somewhere between $1 million and $1.5 million in cash that had been hidden in a Littleton storage facility. Jody told him that the money came from a heist, and that he had taken it from a storage facility in North Carolina, and that "if I [Hamilton] ever thought about saying anything to anyone that 'your family and yourself are dead,' " Hamilton testified.

Jennifer Calloway gasped.

"Did you think he was serious?" the prosecutor asked.

"Yes," Hamilton said. He told how, after Jody's arrest, Jennifer had called her husband's business partner to ask him to hide the money. So Hamilton had gone to the storage locker and tried to bury the cash where he hunted in the Rocky Mountains. Then, while Jody Calloway was out on bail and freed from house arrest, he and Hamilton dug up most of the money. Hamilton added that he had kept $68,000 buried, and that he knew he was getting himself in trouble by saying that. But he said he was scared more by what could happen to him if the Calloways were acquitted. He had even finalized his will. "I felt that if they went back to Colorado, my wife, my two boys, and my baby were in danger," he said.

It got worse for the Calloways when Jennifer's sister Jill Shelly testified that the previous night, over dinner, the couple had asked her what she was going to say on the witness stand. The Calloways, she said, asked her to lie in court and testify she had paid them $700 a month in rent while living in an Arizona condo they owned; her rent money presumably would explain some extra cash the Calloways had on hand. But Shelly had never actually paid them rent—only utilities, fees, and taxes. Shelly told her husband about the conversation. He then called the authorities. "He told me the truth was the best possible way," she said. "This is very hard."

Judge Richard Voorhees had heard enough. The Calloways' bonds were revoked, and they were handcuffed and led to jail. They unsuccessfully begged the judge to reconsider.

The next day's testimony revolved around their Colorado lifestyle.

Their old landlord testified that when Jody Calloway moved to Littleton from North Carolina in January 1998, he paid rent six months in advance.

A man told how he received $4,500 in cash and a $4,000 cashier's check for a boat he sold Jennifer in May 1998.

Later, the Calloways had bought a nearby house. They agreed to a purchase price of $212,000, putting $50,000 down in October 1998. Living in North Carolina, Jody and Jennifer had one vehicle. In Colorado, they had five.

And in a startling piece of evidence, Jody's and Jennifer's former North Carolina employers showed the similar resignation letters written in December 1997, each one saying the writer was resigning because the spouse was being transferred. Neither was actually transferred, their then-supervisors testified.

Meanwhile, FBI agents used Joseph Hamilton's testimony as a map to find more of the missing money. Over the weekend, they discovered $68,000 buried in a tin ammunition container on a mountain near Denver, Colorado, and $10,000 in the ceiling of Hamilton's workshop in Littleton. Agents flew the money to Charlotte so prosecutors would have it in court on the next day of testimony.

But as it turned out, there was no need for more evidence. On Saturday, August 25, the Calloways and their lawyers decided that the defendants' best bet would be guilty pleas. Early on Monday, August 27, 2001, they pleaded guilty to money laundering and receiving stolen property. They angered authorities when they said they didn't know where the remaining unspent portion of their loot was.

The jury members had not heard Hamilton's testimony and didn't know about the guilty pleas until they were already entered. Some laughed. Others stared at the money bag containing $78,000, which sat on the prosecutor's table.

Kathy Grigg continued to maintain she was not guilty of possession of stolen property involving the disputed $28,000. The prosecutor charged her with perjury. She agreed to plead guilty in return for the feds' dropping the larceny charge. But she then told *Charlotte Observer* reporter Aileen Soper that she was actually innocent. When the feds read the newspaper story, they asked a judge to reverse her guilty plea. The judge agreed. She went to trial for perjury and lost.

The sentences of Jody and Jennifer Calloway figured to be about five years, longer than those given to most defendants from the earlier rounds of heist arrests, because the others received leniency for pleading guilty. The Calloways' and Kathy Grigg's time away would begin about five years after the heist. Their closest connections to the original theft, Nathan and Amy Grant, were already out of prison.

Still in prison were Steve Chambers, David Ghantt, Kelly Campbell, Michele Chambers, Jeff Guller, Eric Payne, and Scott Grant.

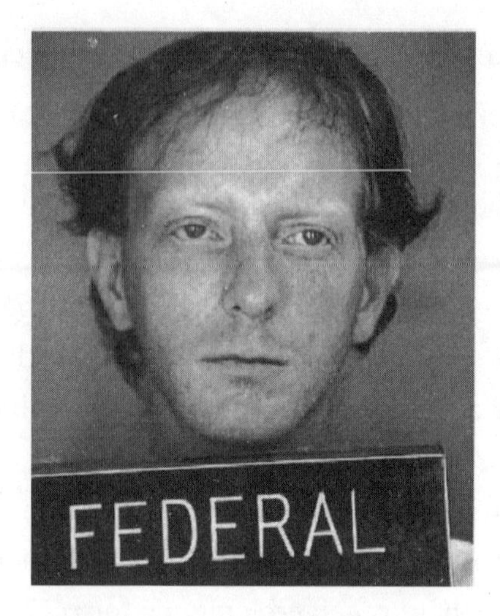

David Ghantt
Charlotte Observer

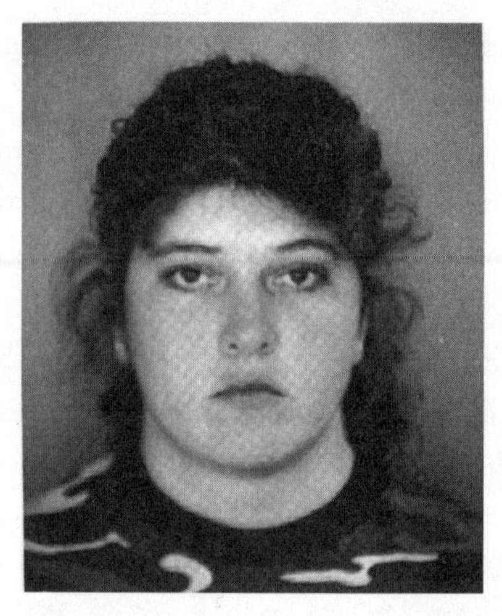

Kelly Campbell
Charlotte Observer

Epilogue

Nothing has symbolized the lunacy of the heist saga like the legend of the velvet Elvis.

It did not matter that this legend's origin was false, that Steve and Michele did not actually buy the chintzy piece and did not defile their luxury home by hanging it prominently. The velvet Elvis was already in the house when they moved in, a gag gift for the previous homeowners from their relatives. But Steve and Michele's ownership of it seemed to tip the case's public absurdity scale. The air was already heavy with tales of mindless extravagance and plastic surgery. Carolinians who followed heist news during the late 1990s cared little about the truth behind the velvet Elvis, because the legend was more fun to believe.

That's why, at the auction in February 1999, it sold for $1,600. Tom Law wanted both a piece of heist history and good advertising, and he knew the velvet Elvis would be the best conversation piece in the city. It has hung behind the counter at his Charlotte shop, Ameri-

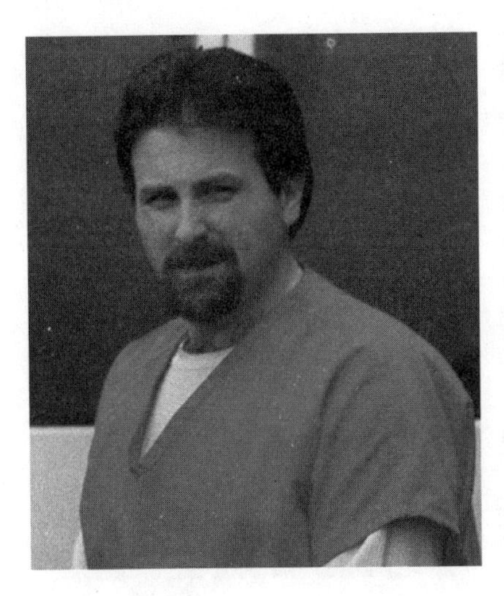

Steve Chambers
CHARLOTTE OBSERVER

Michele Chambers
CHARLOTTE OBSERVER

can Gun and Pawn, since the auction. "I've had people say, 'I won't do any business with any other pawnshop but you, because you've got the velvet Elvis,' " he said in April 2002. "I got offered $6,000 for it. But it's not for sale. I get such a big kick out of it."

The Loomis Fargo heist was not a victimless crime. The defendants' families suffered, and Loomis Fargo lost money and was embarrassed by a second huge heist in a single year. Still, there was no violence, so people felt free to laugh at Steve and Michele's extravagance, at David Ghantt's tropical dreams and naiveté, and at the other defendants' bumbling. That's why, when Law bought the velvet Elvis, he was treated like a celebrity, "like I was the head draft pick for the Charlotte Hornets. Everyone patted me on the shoulder."

Could the plot have succeeded? Would more polished behavior have allowed the gang to get away with it? Short of killing people to eliminate witnesses, could anyone steal and spend that much money without getting caught?

Some of the answers seem obvious. The defendants could have

Scott Grant
CHARLOTTE OBSERVER

Nathan Grant
CHARLOTTE OBSERVER

moved far away. They could have involved fewer people. They could have spent less. Had they been willing to leave the area instead of immediately buying a $635,000 home so close to the scene of the crime, maybe they could have quietly started new lives, perhaps even as big spenders, without creating headlines. Even if they elected to stay in the Charlotte region, they could have waited to change residences. The temptation to spend was undoubtedly great, but patience would have been an easier course than the alternative—prison.

I never learned directly from Steve Chambers why he stayed near Charlotte. People who knew him said it was mainly because he wanted to show off to people who knew him.

Given the reluctance of Kelly and Steve to move far away and assume new identities, the crime effort was doomed when the FBI learned soon after the heist that Kelly probably had a relationship with David Ghantt. There was nothing the gang could have done about that, because Ghantt had told some colleagues he was dating Kelly.

David may have known a few things about the FBI, but he appar-

Eric Payne
Charlotte Observer

Mike McKinney
Charlotte Observer

ently did not know the agents would pump his coworkers and former coworkers the way they did. Had he realized that before the heist, maybe he would have reconsidered Kelly's invite and either rejected the whole idea, recruited somebody else himself, or taken a manageable load in a few bags and driven out west.

Given her connection to David, there was no way Kelly could have stayed in Gaston County and enjoyed the money in a way to make the theft worthwhile for her. The FBI was watching her.

Perhaps Steve could have fled with the cash or bought his big house in a different time zone, but short of killing Kelly and David, he had no way to ensure they would not squeal. He, too, could have sat on the money, or at least spent it less quickly. But even had he done so, the FBI would still have watched Kelly, and he would have had to keep a strict distance from her.

Steve's cousins also hurt his chances. While abandoning the Loomis van on the night of the theft, Scott Grant left its ignition running though Steve wanted him to turn it off, so a passerby might drive it elsewhere and lead the FBI astray. The future wife of his other cousin, Nathan Grant, unwittingly brought Jody and Jennifer Calloway into the picture.

David Ghantt was not apologetic. When I interviewed him in prison, he said he felt bad about upsetting his wife and family but not about the act itself or the bad publicity it caused Loomis Fargo, which he felt worked him too hard for too little money. "I'm not gonna be like the other people, crying and weeping about how sorry they are. That's fake. . . . What's the point? I made a choice, a decision. It was a calculated risk. I guess that makes me a bastard of sorts."

He referred to his five months on the run as the most exciting time of his life. And he appreciated that some of his experiences would read well. He enjoyed telling me about listening to the radio while driving to work in his truck on the morning of the crime. "They were playing 'Take the Money and Run,' " he said. "I shit you not."

Once, when asked about his hobbies as a child, he replied that he was a bit of an oddball growing up, having been more interested in reading about different cultures than playing or following sports. "I like history," he said, "just seeing how people used to do things. It's fascinating. I like to think, 'Why did General Lee go to Gettysburg? How did the Egyptians build the pyramids? Why did civilizations fall?' I would try to discuss these things with my school friends, and they would look at me like I was stupid or something. They were collecting baseball cards. I couldn't have told them who was on first, but I could've told them who the Egyptian god of the dead was."

"Who," I asked him, in prison, "was the Egyptian god of the dead?"

"Enobus," David answered confidently.

I checked later, and he was correct.

Kelly Campbell, echoing several other defendants in the case, said the biggest lesson she learned from the heist was that money was not as important as she once thought, that in the end, it was family that was most important. What she regretted most, she said, was her time in prison away from her children.

She said she felt guilty about her involvement in the murder plot, and that she was trying to forgive Steve. "I had a lot of hostility toward him right after the arrest, when I found out all the lies he had told me," she revealed to the *Charlotte Observer*. "I am trying to live life as a Christian now, and you can't hold hate in your heart and live for the Lord. I don't think we'll ever be friends like we used to be, but I've forgiven him for everything."

Steve Chambers declined my repeated requests for interviews. Information on his background was available in his testimony at two trials, court documents, transcripts, and summaries of recorded phone calls. Interviews with people who knew him provided a glimpse into his mind-set.

In August 1998, he agreed through his then-attorney, Chris Fialko, to answer a small list of general questions that the *Charlotte Observer* submitted in writing. The *Observer* then published his answers. Asked about his biggest lessons from the experience, he responded, "I've learned that family is more important and valuable than money, and that my love for my family is by far the most important thing in my life. I think I always knew that, but lost my way for a while." Asked what it was like to live on Cramer Mountain, he responded, "It was not exciting. It was too complicated and wasn't worth it at all. I wish it hadn't happened."

The first time I interviewed Michele Chambers, she offered to show me her implants, of which she was very proud. I politely declined, figuring more harm than good would come of it. I would have learned that she had a heart tattoo on her left breast. I didn't find that out until later, while reading court documents that detailed her physical description after her arrest.

Jeff Guller said he felt railroaded. He believed that, in the scheme of things, he was treated worse than the others who were convicted. Not only was his prison sentence longer than Kelly's and David's, but he effectively lost a legal career. He said the only reason he was in prison was because his client happened to be involved in a $17 million heist, and that he did not do anything in 1997 or 1998 that was worse than what many lawyers commonly did without penalty. He said he planned to reapply for his legal license when freed but doubted he would practice law again. Instead, he thought he might try becoming a counselor for other defendants, to help them through the court system.

He remained furious at the FBI and the prosecutors. "I'm angry," he said. "And I don't want to not be angry. I want to be angry at those motherfuckers for the rest of my life."

What of the defendants as a group?

First of all, if you work in a courthouse, whether as a lawyer or a clerk or a reporter, you see worse people than most of these defendants almost every day. True, Steve Chambers had a long history of criminal behavior, but the rest of the defendants had few, if any, serious legal transgressions until the heist and its aftermath.

That is not to say they didn't deserve criminal charges. Between October 4, 1997, and March 2, 1998, they did a number of unsavory or inappropriate things. And while David Ghantt certainly had reason to see himself as a pawn, that did not change the fact that he very willingly stole $17 million, that he took it from a trusting employer, that he did it intending to not give it back, and that he abandoned his family, including a wife who depended on him.

Less than six months after the heist, the FBI had arrested seventeen people and found most of the stolen money. Four years after the heist, it had arrested twenty-four people, all of whom were convicted, and located or accounted for more than 95 percent of the stolen cash. As of 2002, about $14.1 million of the $17 million had been recovered. The companies hoped to recover a portion of the remaining $2.9 million—most of which the defendants spent while free after the heist—through restitution payments and by retrieving approximately $700,000 that they believed was somewhere in Colorado.

Still, at parties around town, FBI agents heard comments along the lines of, "How could you *not* have made those arrests? Those people were so *stupid*!"

How tough was the investigation?

Given the defendants' outlandish behavior, it is tempting to think the agents could have achieved similar results by sitting at their desks and waiting for the confidential informants to call. But actually, their investigative work developed leads that prepared them to pounce when relevant tips came in from informants.

The FBI started with a big tip because, security cameras or not, company officials would have told them David Ghantt worked at Loomis Fargo that day. Still, early that week, exhaustive FBI interviews quickly identified Kelly Campbell as a former Loomis employee, a possible Ghantt girlfriend, and a potential accomplice. That interview work led to surveillance. After a confidential informant identified Steve Chambers to the FBI, it became significant that Kelly and Steve spent time together, that she bought a minivan under Steve's alias, and that their telephone records indicated contact.

Across the country, it is not hard to find examples of law-enforcement investigations in which detectives' inadequate planning or wrong turns hinder them in a case. Even during the successful Loomis investigation, a telephone call soon after the heist from Jeff Guller's office aide to *America's Most Wanted*—a call that could have expedited the investigation—fell through the cracks.

Of course, the confidential informants were helpful. Some observers doubted he deserved it, but Steve's old friend from Belmont Hosiery brought home a $250,000 reward, making him the biggest recipient of Loomis award money. The man who spotted the abandoned Loomis van the day after the theft came away with $25,000. Other awards also were distributed.

As for the agents themselves, Mark Rozzi, already a specialist in bank-robbery investigations, became sought after as a speaker in investigators' circles. John Wydra began drawing quips from North Carolina defense attorneys along the lines of, "I know where my client's money came from, John, and it's clean," a reference to Jeff Guller's situation. He oversaw an FBI team that sifted through rubble at the Pentagon in the weeks following September 11, 2001. Dick Womble retired in January 2000 and spent a year as a traveling security consultant for the NBA's Charlotte Hornets.

As for the prosecutors, David Keesler and Brian Whisler considered bringing charges against other people with lesser roles, but they decided government money would be better spent pursuing other cases. They were presented United States Justice Department awards from Attorney General Janet Reno in 1999 for their work prosecuting the case.

A main security goal at armored-car companies is to have two people working at a time with large amounts of cash. That's why the trucks' security apparatuses typically take two people to open. That way, the industry theory goes, a company does not have to put too much trust in one person.

Loomis Fargo had two people working on October 4, 1997. One was a trainee, which David Ghantt seemed to count on. During the hiring process, company employees have to pass honesty tests, drug tests, and criminal-background checks. Still, the company lost nearly $39 million from inside jobs in 1997—$17 million in the Charlotte heist, $18.8 million in Philip Noel Johnson's, and $3 million in an Oklahoma theft.

"Enforcement procedures are in place, and that's going to stop a lot of it, but you're not going to stop all of it," said Pat Flaherty, a Loomis Fargo spokesman, in the *Florida Times-Union* on October 7, 1997. "Historically, it happens. Batters go through streaks where they're hot and when they're not. This is just not a good streak for us right now."

Over time, people who manage to steal millions of dollars usually get caught. That was true even before David Ghantt went to work on October 4, 1997. Regardless, some people think they can get away with anything.

"It was kind of an ego thing," David said in a December 2001 prison interview. "I knew [that] when I did this, I would be famous. I knew it would create a big stir. The thought of that, I think, drives a lot of crimes. People want the fifteen minutes of fame. I doubt my place in the history books will be that big, but people will know me for a while."

We finished the interview and shook hands. I left, and he was led back to the prison's general circulation area.

Acknowledgments

I WANT TO THANK THE PEOPLE involved in the theft and its aftermath who trusted their stories to me. I hope they, and the others, feel this book treats them fairly. I also want to thank the investigators and prosecutors who shared their experiences.

Other people to thank, for various reasons, include literary agent Agnes Birnbaum; editor Steve Kirk; Carolyn Sakowski; Michaela Hamilton; Philip Gerard; Noell Tin; James Gronquist; Chris Fialko; Ashley Tillman; James Dunbar; Sean Steele; Scott Huseby; Cheryl Nuccio; Dr. Philip and Julie Weiss; Judy and David Taylor of Advanced Bonding Warehouse; Steve Gladden; Harold Bender; Joel Bartow; Jackie Taylor; Michael McGee; Tim Hass; Gary Boyd; the Gaston County court clerks; the court clerks at the federal courthouse in Charlotte; Larry Wiley; *Charlotte Observer* reporters and editors, including Joe DePriest, Chip Wilson, Carolyn Murray, Cheryl Carpenter, Anna Griffin, and Aileen Soper; *Star-Ledger* reporters and editors including Kevin Coughlin, Mark Di Ionno, Rebecca Goldsmith, and Steve Liebman; Gila and Adam Schwartz; Cathy Schenker; Eric Chun; Jennifer Hillygus;

Phil Clark; David Leonhardt; Ben Madley; and Charles Hill. I also thank the officials at the Mecklenburg County Jail and at the federal prisons in Butner, North Carolina; Alderson, West Virginia; and Estill, South Carolina. Lastly, I thank my first editors, to whom this book is dedicated: Stephanie Platzman, my brother Eric, and my parents.

Index